THE CHURCH
IN PLURALIST
SOCIETY

SOCIAL AND POLITICAL ROLES

EDITED BY
CORNELIUS J. CASEY
AND FÁINCHE RYAN

University of Notre Dame Press
Notre Dame, Indiana

University of Notre Dame Press
Notre Dame, Indiana 46556
undpress.nd.edu
Copyright © 2019 by the University of Notre Dame

Published in the United States of America

Library of Congress Control Number: 2019952785

ISBN: 978-0-268-10641-6 (Hardback)
ISBN: 978-0-268-10642-3 (Paperback)
ISBN: 978-0-268-10644-7 (WebPDF)
ISBN: 978-0-268-10643-0 (Epub)

THE CHURCH IN PLURALIST SOCIETY

CONTENTS

PREFACE

The church in every age has to ask questions of its own identity and mission. To this task it brings a long tradition of self-understanding. The Second Vatican Council (1962–65), an extensive corporate exploration of these issues, became a sign of ecclesial strength and health in the Holy Spirit. Rowan Williams, former archbishop of Canterbury and Cambridge academic, noted that the council was "a sign of promise, a sign that the Church was strong enough to ask itself some demanding questions about whether its culture and structures were adequate to the task of sharing the gospel with the complex, often rebellious, always restless mind of the modern world."[1]

The authoritative documents that emerged, in particular *Dignitatis Humanae* and *Gaudium et Spes*, effectively represent a radical shift from a positioning of the church in Western culture that had prevailed for many centuries. *Dignitatis Humanae* offered a new understanding of the role of the Catholic Church vis-à-vis political and state authorities. In *Gaudium et Spes* the target was bigger, concern was wider. It can be read as an attempt to interpret the stance of the church in relation to the whole project of modernity, the whole structure of modern civilization.

New horizons came into view. They have served as points of departure. In the intervening period, several pathways have been, and are being, explored. Some people manifest unease, asking whether we can find a way back to the safety of the earlier eras. Others wonder whether new ways cannot be tried out more vigorously. It is inevitable that there is some adversarial element in such explorations, but it is scarcely sufficient to leave the matter at that. It is important to ask if we are listening to a cacophony of voices, each crying its truth from its own silo, or if we listen more deeply might we discern the symphony which is the truth of the Catholic Church in these times.

This collection of essays offers a sustained reflection on the church's identity and mission. Its fundamental presumption is that it is timely, indeed imperative, to keep alive the question of the church's self-understanding as it continues to journey alongside "the complex, often rebellious, always restless mind of the modern world." The focus is largely the Catholic Church in the Western world, but there are key points that cross over with relevance to other ecclesial contexts.

The contributors come from a range of disciplines: public policy, literary theory, political theory, sociology, theology, philosophy, and church history. They do not all have the same approach to the role of the church. It may be that it is precisely the ability to hear this diversity that is crucial for the health of the church in our time.

The opening chapter, "Church-World and Church-State: The Journey since Vatican II," by J. Bryan Hehir, underlines the importance of the perspectives brought to light by Vatican II. It offers a convincing and resounding argument that pluralism is here to stay and that the church should welcome this. The task of Catholicism is to work with pluralism intelligently and effectively. Hehir articulates how the church in a pluralist society can be conceived both as a corporate body with its own identity and as one with the institutional resources to cooperate with state institutions in providing education, health, and other resources for human flourishing.

If one accepts the assertion that pluralism is here to stay, it is important to recognize that the notion of pluralism is not wholly unproblematic. Terry Eagleton offers a provocative reflection in the second chapter, "Against Pluralism." The Christian gospel, he reminds us, is about critique rather than conformity. This critique must be directed to the idea of pluralism in modern ideologies. One of the more disreputable reasons, Eagleton argues, that pluralism is part of the dominant ideology of contemporary Western civilizations is that truth seeking in such a climate doesn't really matter all that much. Against this, he points out that the Christian gospel is a relentlessly uncompromising affair. Truth in its eyes is not in the end pluralistic and many sided. It is a cutting sword: either you fed the hungry or you didn't. Difference and diversity are not as vital as our common humanity in Christ.

From a different perspective, in "Hegemonic Liberalism and the End of Pluralism," Patrick J. Deneen claims that contemporary society is becoming less pluralistic and diverse and far more homogeneous and standardized. He demonstrates that a certain ideology of liberalism has become dominant in Western society. This liberalism, he argues, is aggressively powered by economic forces and by the reach of global corporate consumerism. The ideology of liberalism is crowding out and marginalizing alternative visions of human flourishing. Deneen's thesis is that the church should position itself as an alternative, countercultural corporate body, remaining in touch with its wisdom.

A large presence in many of the essays is Charles Taylor and his magisterial work, *A Secular Age*. This is particularly the case in the contributions of Hans Joas and William T. Cavanaugh, who face the challenge of secularism most frontally. In doing so, however, they are not simply derivative of Taylor, but make useful contributions of their own. One of the consequences of the rise of the secular option analyzed by Taylor is that faith itself has become an option in the West. This means that faith today is permeated with the awareness that the option for a secular narrative for human flourishing is readily available. This drastically changes the preconditions for Christian faith. From different perspectives both Joas and Cavanaugh engage with this cultural phenomenon. In "The Church in a World of Options," Joas addresses this question from a sociological perspective. He explores models of the church that could be attractive and illuminating in this changed world. Cavanaugh argues in "The Church's Place in a Consumer Society: The Hegemony of Optionality" that the paradox of optionality is that optionality is not optional but has become hegemonic. For Cavanaugh the privileging of choice as the supreme cultural value and motivating factor leads in effect to a paralysis of deeper human freedoms. Without due care the church is in danger of being co-opted by the hegemonic forces of optionality and so no longer able to bear witness to its own deeper identity.

Massimo Faggioli takes the discussion in a different direction. He looks at the problem of the established church as it seeks to exercise its mission in contemporary societies. In "The Established Church Dilemma," he notes that many of the structures of the church were forged in another age, which he terms the Constantinian Age. In that epoch, church and state were linked in concordat-like arrangements to mutual benefit. Faggioli notes that an argument can be made that these structures are no longer fit for the church's contemporary mission. However, a study of Pope Francis leads him to argue that while Francis's actions are a clear manifestation of the ecclesiology of the Second Vatican Council, they also draw on structures that were forged in an earlier era. The question for Faggioli is whether it is wise for the church to completely abandon systems that grant it financial support and other special privileges, for it is these very systems that enable the church to fulfill its mission of providing for the poor and the marginalized.

This leads to the question of who makes decisions in the church for the church. The thorny and troublesome question of the loci of ecclesial authority cannot be overlooked. Here again the issue is that of inherited structures and whether they are fit for purpose. This is the question addressed in the penultimate chapter, "'On Consulting the Faithful in Matters of Doctrine': The Twenty-First Century." Fáinche Ryan explores the importance of the *sensus fidei* and the *sensus fidei fidelium* in the life of the church. She argues that the challenge of the contemporary church is to give due operational force to an ecclesiology of the Holy Spirit while at the same time safeguarding the importance of a diversity of leadership and authority roles.

In the challenge of discerning safe routes of passage for the pilgrim church through history, St. Augustine's *City of God* is recognized as a locus classicus. Patrick Riordan's "The Secular Is Not Scary" retrieves an interpretation of Augustine's "two cities" that allows for different kinds of cities and different kinds of engagement with them. He argues that there is room for a form of secularism open to sources of meaning and value that the secular cannot provide for itself. This version of the secular is not scary. It is a potential partner for cooperation with Christian hope.

With its variety of voices, these essays illustrate that any exploration of the role of the church in society in the uncharted waters of the contemporary era is done from within a living tradition. This tradition has carried these questions powerfully forward over many centuries and through many cultures. It is this tradition that gifts the church with its hopeful horizon. The role of the church in a pluralist society is a narrative that is being written by many people at many different levels of the church. They bear witness and testimony in their manifold experience to the church as an institution shaped by the social, political, and cultural forces of their time, yet faithful to its core identity, to be a *Lumen Gentium*, a sacrament of a gift of reconciliation, not just for its internal well-being, but for all of humanity.

The production of this text has been a work of collaboration and dialogue with a variety of people. Particular thanks are due to the generous philanthropic sponsorship that enabled the hosting of a conference on the role of the church in a pluralist society. The idea for this book emerged from the conference. We wish to thank Gerry O'Hanlon, SJ, Patrick Hannon, Maria Duffy, Jean Callanan, Helen McMahon, Peg Masterson, Denis Casey, John Kelly, Barbara Fitzgerald, and our colleagues at the Loyola Institute. We thank the Loyola Trust for financial help in editing the book, as well as for their support of the conference.[2] In addition, the assistance of Máire Ní Chearbhaill, Brendan McConvery, CSsR, and Raphael Gallagher, CSsR, was indispensable.

NOTES

1. Rowan Williams, *Holy Living: The Christian Tradition for Today* (London: Bloomsbury, 2017), 93.

2. The founding of the Loyola Institute was made possible by the generosity and vision of a confederation of religious congregations (Augustinians, Carmelites [O.Carm]), Columbans, Jesuits, Loreto Sisters, Marists, Oblates, Society of African Missions) and the College authorities in the University of Dublin, Trinity College Dublin.

ONE

Church-World and Church-State

The Journey since Vatican II

J. BRYAN HEHIR

Within a single civil society there are individuals and communities who hold profoundly different convictions about the ultimate questions of life. The challenge of religious pluralism, therefore, is twofold: first, how to protect the human and civil right of religious freedom (i.e., the freedom to believe or abstain from belief and the freedom to believe in diverse ways); and second, how to fashion basic agreement on the moral content of law and policy that will shape the lives of all members of the society. Pluralism takes on a different character in differing political systems, but the basic meaning and challenges it poses maintain consistency across societies and cultures. This chapter focuses on how the Catholic Church engages pluralism by drawing on three resources: its theology of church-world relations, its doctrine of church and state, and its social teaching of the past century.[1]

The method of the chapter moves in three steps: a brief comparison of the history and character of the three resources, an analysis of the documents of the Second Vatican Council and subsequent developments, and an example of the church engaging pluralism in the United States.

ENGAGING PLURALISM: THREE RESOURCES

The three resources have different histories, and they respond to distinct but related questions. Only a brief comparison is possible here. The church-world question is rooted in the New Testament. It asks about the meaning Christians and the church should attach to the world in its temporal, contingent but complex dimensions: its intellectual life and learning; its politics, economy, and material developments; and its achievements in diverse fields over the ages. The meaning and value given these dimensions of life is then complemented by the judgments made about how to define the working relationships of Christian faith and morals for the world of each age.

It is possible, I believe, to distinguish three meanings of "the world" in Catholic theology. First, there is the world of the material cosmos that Christians understand in terms of the doctrine of creation but also in terms of the incarnation. At this first level the world is understood in a positive fashion. Creation is the work of God, requires human stewardship, and invites the use of human intelligence and skill in probing and expanding its potential.

Second, in both the Christian scriptures and in theological assessment there is a depiction of the world as a threat and danger to the Christian ideal for the world. The first epistle of John warns the disciples to avoid "the world, the flesh and the devil." In his Last Supper discourse in John's gospel, Jesus warns his closest followers that they are not "of the world" and can expect hatred from the world. The world here is not the cosmos but rather the world as it has been shaped by sin in its multiple personal and social expressions. This conception of the world promises constant struggle and opposition throughout history. The third meaning of the world is the most complex and the most relevant to our discussion of pluralism. Here the world is where the disciples should be, but being "in the world" involves continuing choices, decisions, and commitments. The tension in this more complex understanding of "the world" is reflected in the Last Supper discourse where Jesus prays that the disciples remain in the world testifying to the truth and in need of the Father's protection of them.

The combinations of the three meanings of the world frame a Christian understanding of the church vis-à-vis the world. The material creation in all its potential should be preserved, developed, and rendered useful for the flourishing of the human family. Christians should be among those engaging and leading this process across the spectrum of human creativity in all its forms, from manual labor to intellectual life to multiple secular occupations in the private and public sectors. Finally, the work of transforming the world inevitably encounters the double obstacles of human limitation and sin.

Pope John XXIII encouraged this engagement in *Pacem in Terris*, and Pope John Paul II in *Laborem Exercens* boldly described human work in all its forms as cooperation with and imitation of God's creative activity. Preserving and developing the material creation in our time is a more complex challenge than it once was for two reasons. First, the human capacity for innovation, invention, and—uniquely in our time—cultivation of the process of globalization has opened avenues of change in human life within societies and globally to a degree unknown in recorded history. Within less than a century human intelligence, science, and technology have combined to split the atom, crack the genetic code, and pierce the veil of space. These developments, and others like them, mean that questions that on the surface appear to be purely political, economic, or bio-medical have a deeper moral core. These questions are always empirically complex, but that is matched by their moral complexity.

Second, as the frontiers of what is possible in the world have been relentlessly pushed back, a new awareness has emerged about respect for creation, for the environment that forms the context on which life depends. Being "in the world," fulfilling the human and Christian vocation to care for and develop the potential of the world, requires continuing recognition of what can be done in the world and what should never be done.[2]

This Christian vision of the world, the third meaning of "world," was captured by *Gaudium et Spes* in this way:

> The world which the council has in mind is the world of women
> and men, the entire human family seen in its total environment. It is

the world as the theatre of human history, bearing the marks of its travail, its triumphs and failures. It is the world which the Christians believe has been created and is sustained by the love of its maker, has fallen into the slavery of sin but has been freed by Christ, who was crucified and rose again in order to break the stranglehold of the evil one, so that it might be fashioned anew according to God's design and brought to its fulfillment.[3]

Fashioning the world anew is what the church-world question is about. To fulfill this task the other two resources of Catholic thought are needed. The church-state question emerged only slightly later than the church-world encounter. As the early Christian community took shape in the context of the Roman Empire, tension and conflict seemed inevitable. The problem lay in the way each entity, empire and church, defined its identity. Rome, the dominant political force in the ancient world, was solidly tied to the classical idea that the polis was the supreme political and legal authority in its expansive territory. Other aspects of society, the family, the economy, and religion, were to be subordinated to the polis. This conception touched the lives of individuals and families directly; it involved military service for the empire and also emperor worship. The church, based on the understanding of its identity—including the dictum that "we must obey God rather than men"—brought two claims against the scope of the emperor's authority and legitimacy.

The first was a claim of conscience; the early church was convinced that dictates of the state were subject to review by the higher wisdom they found in the Word of God. To make the claim was dangerous; for many it meant martyrdom. But it posed an alternative voice for one community of Roman citizens, and this was profoundly destabilizing for the state. The second claim was an assertion of the public identity of the church. It claimed public space within the empire because it understood its origin, destiny, and mission to be derived independently of the state. The classical statement of the claim to independence and public identity was Pope Gelasius's letter to the emperor Anastasius, defining the "two swords" theory of political and spiritual authority.[4] Unlike the theological discourse on the church-world question, best exemplified in Augustine's *City of God*, that on church and state quickly took the form of institutional and legal arguments, rooted in theological premises to be sure but focused on line-drawing issues of legitimacy and authority and law.

While the church-world question has been about the theological-moral imperatives defining the mission and ministry of the church, the church-state agenda had two principal topics: first, how church and state should collaborate in the service of a common constituency, the person who is both citizen and Christian; and second, how to defend the church's existence, and freedom to function, when the state has assumed a hostile or dominating posture. From the empire to the medieval commonwealth to the modern state, church-state issues have remained central for Catholicism.

Both the church-state and church-world questions have had a longer history than what has come to be called in the past century Catholic social teaching. Dating from the pontificate of Leo XIII (1878–1903) through Pope Francis (2013–), the era of social teaching has drawn on the deeper categories of Catholic theology and jurisprudence and developed a distinctive style. The style has been shaped by the papacy; the social teaching is broader than the papal teaching but has found its principal expression in a stream of papal encyclicals and addresses. Over the course of the past 125 years these papal letters to the church and the world manifest two characteristics: an expanding scope of subject matter and a changing mode of discourse. The social tradition began focused on the plight of nations addressing social justice and socioeconomic issues; this focus consumed the first half century of the encyclical tradition. In the next seventy-five years both the issues addressed and the level of analysis changed substantially. The level of analysis moved beyond the nation-state and has increasingly addressed the international system in the forms it has assumed since the end of World War II. This broader horizon includes nuclear weapons and modern warfare, human rights (including the right to religious freedom), international social justice, and—most recently—the environment.

In expanding its range, post–Vatican II social teaching has increasingly moved from the principally philosophical style of analysis and expression (using natural law as its method) to a mix of philosophical and theological ideas and discourse. This more evangelical style has both deepened the analysis within the ecclesial community and narrowed its audience to some degree. The discussion of which categories should shape the church's address to the world is an ongoing, useful one in Catholicism today.

VATICAN II: THE EVENT AND ITS IMPACT

The Second Vatican Council (1962–65) has had deep and powerful consequences for the whole life and ministry of the Catholic Church. The council was an ecclesiological event, examining systematically the life of the church *ad intra et ad extra*.[5] In retrospect it can be argued that no area of the church's ministry was more powerfully changed than its public and social role. In part the reason for this was the way in which the council purposefully moved away from the posture of Catholicism toward the world that had dominated the eighteenth and nineteenth centuries. This change of direction, begun at the council and continuing into our own time, was accomplished only with great struggle intellectually and organizationally. Some of the most complex debates at Vatican II were about the effort to leave the public legacy of Pius IX and the "Syllabus of Errors" behind. The two documents of the council that sparked the debate and that symbolized the change were *Dignitatis Humanae* (Declaration on Religious Freedom) and *Gaudium et Spes* (The Pastoral Constitution on the Church in the Modern World).[6] Neither document was focused directly on religious and moral pluralism, but both of them have powerfully shaped the way in which the church (institutionally and as a community) has understood pluralism and responded to it. The "journey since Vatican II" cited in my title was catalyzed by these two texts, and both continue to be central points of reference as the church engages the world more than fifty years later. The journey has moved beyond the texts themselves but not away from them. It is particularly necessary to recognize that the response of the church to pluralism in the world has sparked a pluralist response within the church. Responding to pluralism has meant different things in Poland and the Philippines, in South Africa and South Korea, in Paris and Lagos, in London and Santiago.[7]

Here I examine the conciliar texts themselves and draw out the implications that flow from them. Particular case studies of the pluralism within the church lie beyond the limits of this chapter, but the texts and the themes that have been incarnated in diverse local churches and in the papacy itself can be identified.

Dignitatis Humanae

As the council opened, one of the most awaited and expected statements in the wider world was about the topic of religious freedom. The principal reasons for this were, first, the fact that the topic was central to pluralism in societies and across national boundaries; and second, Catholicism, in its church-state teaching, had staunchly resisted any change in its way of addressing either religious freedom or pluralism. The Catholic response remained committed to a policy of toleration embodied in the formula "thesis–hypothesis." Basically this meant that the expectation of the church in Catholic countries was a position of establishment, or favored status, with limits on the public expression of faith by other religious groups.

The expectation that change would occur at Vatican II was multidimensional: theological analysis had moved to a different position within the church; ecumenical observers at the council represented the weight the Protestant communities gave to this issue; and in international law, the concept of religious freedom had acquired a secure status through the UN Declaration on Human Rights. It may be surprising in retrospect that with this attention focused on the issues, it still took all four sessions of Vatican II, right up to its final months, to have a document accepted by the council.

The primary reason, specified by the principal author of the text, John Courtney Murray, SJ, was not only the embedded position of "thesis–hypothesis," but the fact that change in that formula raised the large issue of how doctrine can develop within Catholicism (or, for some, whether it can or should develop). The conciliar text specified this complex challenge in its opening paragraphs: "In dealing with this question of liberty the sacred Council intends to develop the teaching of recent popes on the inviolable rights of the human person and on the constitutional order of society" (*Dignitatis Humanae* 1, hereafter *DH*).

This serenely stated objective left unstated the scope of the task "to develop the doctrine" in any area of Catholic teaching. In one of his many commentaries on the final text, Murray identified the three broad areas that *Dignitatis Humanae* engaged: (1) the ethical issue of religious freedom; (2) the political issue of the role of the state in religious questions; and (3) the theological issue of freedom of the church in Catholic teaching.

Taken together these three themes effected a basic change in Catholic teaching on religious freedom and on church-state relations. The core of the conciliar document is simple and direct: "The Vatican Council declares that the human person has a right to religious freedom" (*DH* 2). It then provided in succinct terms the basis of this judgment, the content of the right, and the limits of the exercise of the right.[8] The basis of the right is the dignity of the human person. The content of the right is immunity from coercion in religious matters; no one is to be forced to believe, and none are to be prevented from expressing their beliefs in public. In addition, the right extends beyond individuals to religious communities. In the exercise of their religious rights individuals and communities are limited only by the requirements of public order: that is, public peace, requirements of justice, and public morality.[9] Each of these elements in the definition can be played out in much more detail, but they summarize the council's view of religious freedom.

To complement this definition, the conciliar text stresses the responsibilities and the limits of the state's role regarding religion. Basically, the state's primary responsibility is to protect the right of religious freedom for each person; beyond that religious communities are responsible for the religious character of the society, not the state. Finally, in a significant change, *Dignitatis Humanae* asserts that the basic principle in church-state relations is the freedom of the church to function.[10] In the past, the Catholic "thesis" sought a privileged position for the church. No longer: this change left the church the challenge of establishing trust in pluralistic societies and being persuasive in its teaching and advocacy.

How should the consequences of *Dignitatis Humanae* be evaluated? First, a limited, specific change in Catholic teaching extended far beyond the precise object of the text. Second, the conciliar statement filled a recognized gap in Catholic teaching on human rights. Catholicism had a conflicted relationship with the emergence of the modern conception of human rights; substantial philosophical issues created tension with secular human rights discourse. Beginning with Pius XII (1939–58) and uniquely with John XXIII's encyclical *Pacem in Terris* (1963), substantial

Catholic engagement on human rights lessened the tension.[11] But even in *Pacem in Terris* a right to religious freedom was asserted but not argued. The conciliar text provided a concise rationale for how the church viewed human dignity, human rights, and then religious freedom as one of the political-civil rights of the person.

Third, the brief but specific treatment of the role of the state allowed the church to affirm the secularity and appropriate secular autonomy of the state in society. This affirmation opened the way for the church to recognize and accept various forms of "separation" of religion and the state as the basis for cooperation.

Fourth, having affirmed the secularity of the state, the church in turn recognized in the modern era the value of placing some distance between it and the state, whatever form the latter assumed. This too was a shift in perspective and practice. I have argued in other forums that the effect of Vatican II was to render the church less political but more social. The purpose of the distinction was to identify past eras and past practices when concordats and other legal forms of legal establishment could implicate the church in state practices and policies that were morally objectionable. Placing political distance between church and state freed the church to play a broader social role in social advocacy and public policy. In this sense, *Dignitatis Humanae* opened the path for the church to embody the teaching of *Gaudium et Spes*.

Fifth, to affirm the secularity of the state also meant, however, that in its advocacy and social role the church needed to speak a language and create arguments that the state—as secular—could engage. The mode of argument that begins with "thus saith the Lord" can be used, but it also can be less effective precisely because of the state's secularity.

Sixth and finally, as noted above, *Dignitatis Humanae* affirmed one single principle for the church in addressing the state: not favoritism but freedom. The freedom to function in its teaching, advocacy, and public role corresponded to the church's sense of itself in the conciliar teaching, a servant church and a pilgrim people in history.

Gaudium et Spes

While *Dignitatis Humanae* was awaited and expected, *Gaudium et Spes* was a total surprise. In the planning for Vatican II multiple drafts on a range of issues were prepared, but there was no plan for a document on the role of the church in the world.[12] The document arose from the debates in the first session of the council. Key bishops from diverse countries regarded the document on the church (*Lumen Gentium*) as insufficient because it concentrated almost exclusively on the internal life of the church. So *Gaudium et Spes* was inaugurated from within the council, and it took the remaining three sessions to garner a consensus on what it should say. There was consensus on a very basic theme: this text should interpret the church to the world. Some argued that it would be different from any other conciliar text in the long history of the church. One of the principal drafters, Archbishop Mark McGrath of Panama, described it as the most original document of the council because "it is the first time a Council has so directly and assiduously addressed itself to the whole broad question of the Church and the temporal order."[13] The topic itself, as noted above, was not new to Catholic theology: *Gaudium et Spes* stood in the line of Augustine's *City of God*. But engaging the issue at the level of an ecumenical council rendered it a different text from the work of theologians throughout history.

In fact, theological reflection in the 1940s and 1950s had prepared the way of the council's work. Yves Congar in his book, *Lay People in the Church*, described two orientations in Catholicism on the topic of church and world.[14] Broadly speaking, they were incarnational humanism and eschatological humanism. The first argued for continuity between human history and eternity and advocated deep involvement by the church in shaping the temporal order; the second perspective stressed a disjunction between human values and human work on the one hand and the future in-breaking of the kingdom of God at the end of time. Congar argued that an integral Catholic perspective required an element of both views, but there was a substantial difference between them. The final version of *Gaudium et Spes* came down quite decisively on the side of incarnational spirituality and ecclesiology.

> We have been warned, of course, that it profits us nothing if
> we gain the whole world and lose or forfeit ourselves. Far from
> diminishing our concern to develop this earth, the expectation of
> a new earth should spur us on, for it is here that the body of a new
> human family grows, foreshadowing in some way the age which is
> to come. That is why, although we must be careful to distinguish

earthly progress clearly from the increase of the kingdom of Christ, such progress is of vital concern to the kingdom of God, insofar as it can contribute to the better ordering of human society. (*GS* 39)

To specify what an incarnational view means, *Gaudium et Spes* used a mix of tone and theology. The style and tone of the text separated it, not only from the nineteenth-century papal positions of Gregory XVI and Pius IX, but also from the more positive positions of Pius XI and Pius XII. *Gaudium et Spes* sought to locate the church squarely in the midst of the world of its time, positioned to offer not only the grace of redemption but also the resources of Catholic engagement to address the major issues facing humanity. From its famous opening paragraph, which tied the church to the hopes and fears, the joys and sorrows of humanity, to its treatment of a range of issues—family, politics, economics, culture, and peace—confronting the world, the church offered her life, teaching, and ministry as a partner with men and women across the globe (*GS* 1). Tone was crucial for *Gaudium et Spes* because it surprised people inside and outside the church. But tone required substance to be convincing: why and how would the change be effected? To that question *Gaudium et Spes* offered its theological view of church and world.

Significantly, the theological starting point was the human person, the identical basis that *Dignitatis Humanae* used. *Gaudium et Spes* asserted that the church should be "the sign and the safeguard of the transcendental dimension of the human person" (*GS* 76). Acting in the service of and in defense of the human person is the way the church fulfills its public role. In a compact section of the text, as Murray explains, *Gaudium et Spes* describes and defends the church's role in the world.[15] It first acknowledges that the church has no unique political charism—no special gift to make political judgments. Here again it affirms the secularity and legitimate autonomy of the state and the political order. It then asserts the church's mission to be religious in nature. But the key step is the next one: it argues that the church should fulfill its religious role in such a way that it realizes four secular functions: defense of the dignity of the person, protection and promotion of human rights, fostering the unity of the human family, and providing a sense of meaning to human activity (*GS* 40–42).

This understanding of how the church should engage the world builds on the changes introduced by *Dignitatis Humanae*. By acknowledging the secularity of the state and by distancing the church from the state, the combined teaching of the two conciliar texts offers the church the basis for an activist social role but not one that depends on special privilege or access to political power and influence. The religious voice arises from civil society; it speaks in terms that the secular state can engage; it addresses issues in the name of the person, not in terms of the interests of the church. This is the realization of the less political but more social role for the church after Vatican II.

Just as *Dignitatis Humanae* generated consequences beyond the specific objective of the text, so *Gaudium et Spes* has had lasting effects on the church and the world.[16] First, the document's tone, style, and substance presented a new posture for the church to engage modernity. "Modernity" here refers to the combined effects of the Reformation, the Renaissance, the Enlightenment, and the democratic revolutions. Previously the Catholic response was simply to oppose each and all; *Gaudium et Spes* sought dialogue, to differentiate what could be compatible with Catholic teaching and what could not. Second, the conciliar text provided a solid theological foundation for the church's social ministry, which increased significantly in the decades following Vatican II. Because of this document the ministry of justice and peace was seen not simply as an extension of the church's principal role, but as embedded in that role.[17]

Third, complementing *Dignitatis Humanae*, this conciliar text affirmed the secularity and proper autonomy of the state and of the intellectual and organizational secularity of society. This allowed both church and state to address major issues from a posture of mutual respect and collaboration. Clear lines made for possible partnerships. Fourth, building on the "incarnational" view of human activity, *Gaudium et Spes* deepened the church's conception of its ministry in the world and broadened its contribution to the world.

PLURALISM AND CATHOLICISM: AN EXAMPLE FROM THE UNITED STATES

The chapter began with an abbreviated definition of the meaning of pluralism and its challenges. In this final section it returns to pluralism, using one example drawn from the United States. The example is meant to be illustrative, not comprehensive, and it is likely to have limited applicability beyond the US constitutional and political system.

The baseline for the case began with Courtney Murray's book *We Hold These Truths: Catholic Reflections on the American Proposition.*[18] This collection of essays examined the Catholic response to pluralism and democracy. It was published in 1960, and it described US pluralism as a four-factored equation: Protestant, Catholic, Jewish, and Secularist participants. At the time I was not aware that anyone disputed Murray's description of the pluralism of the country. However, it cannot account for pluralism today. The equation has expanded and become more complex, with new actors and new issues. Protestantism now is divided into the classic mainline churches and evangelicals; Secularists are growing but again not easily defined; the "Nones" (no organizational affiliation) are not easily collapsed into secularism, and they are increasing rapidly; Catholics exhibit greater pluralism within the church than was true in the 1960s. Islam and Buddhism found no mention in 1960, but both are significant religious communities today.

Murray's philosophical arguments about addressing pluralism in a democracy retain substantial value, but the pluralist arena is different in two ways. The pluralist participants require redefinition in terms of their role, size, and complexity. In addition, the issues Murray identified as challenges remain, but new ones must be addressed. Noticeably among the newer questions are bioethics and sexual and gender issues. Neither were reflected in Murray's work, understandably so. At the time, both were real but hardly visible. Much more space could be used to provide an adequate account of both the old and the new pluralism, but it is cited here as the background to concentrate on a different theme.

One major way in which Catholicism in the United States has engaged pluralism is by using its institutional character. Historically, Catholicism has often been described in terms of its complex internal institutional structure. But the reference here is to the institutions that historically and with high visibility in the United States project Catholicism beyond the boundaries of the church into civil society. Europe was the home and source for many of these institutions. They were adopted and adapted on an expansive scale in the United States in the nineteenth and twentieth centuries. They are focused in three areas: education (preschool through universities), social service, and health care.

These institutions in different ways rely on the resources described in this chapter: they equip the church to engage the world; they depend on church-state guidance and protection; and they exemplify Catholic social teaching not only in words but also in a range of public activities. Each dimension of these Catholic institutions has had a two-stage history.[19] By 1960, when Murray wrote, they all had served principally or exclusively the Catholic population. The way they engaged pluralism was to protect Catholics from it, substantially if not totally. But the 1960s were a turning point in two senses: Vatican II, particularly in *Gaudium et Spes*, called the church to be a sign, light, and leaven in the world. In addition, locally in the United States the Kennedy and Johnson administrations, building on the New Deal of the 1930s, expanded the social role of the federal government. And in the areas of social service and health care they sought institutional partners for the delivery of services. To accept the call of the council and to respond to the US opportunity, the church had to engage pluralism intellectually and institutionally in a new fashion. Institutionally, Catholicism had a unique infrastructure in social service and health care to bring into collaboration with the state. Intellectually, the task was more complex: how to engage secular structures and government funding in a pluralistic society when societal norms did not always reflect deeply held Catholic principles. To frame the question technically, was "moral cooperation" possible, and could "the religious identity" of the institutions be preserved?

Some things were clear. First, to accept the government's invitation meant Catholic institutions had to serve all citizens regardless of religion; the days of an exclusively Catholic clientele were over. Second, federal and state funds could be used only for secular purposes and had to be properly confined to these purposes. Third, government oversight followed government money; transparency was demanded.

For much of the past fifty years the collaboration has been expansive and effective. At the same time collaboration has generated intense debates within the Catholic community and within the wider political community. The former is driven by a small but intense constituency that sees Catholic social service and health care organizations as far too willing to yield to the state and the culture. The latter position, usually secularist in tone, believes firmly that taxpayer dollars should not be enhancing the service capacities of religious groups. These two debates, while real, have usually been contained, or at least limited to, "hard cases" where the line drawn between secular and sacred has been difficult to define. For the most part the secular-sacred partnership on social and health policy has been productive for the society and the ministry of the church. A key element for successful collaboration has been the use of religious exemptions in law and policy: they function by allowing secular law and policies to reflect broadly supported public norms; at the same time they create protective space for religious groups so that their collaboration with the state does not require them to violate deeply held religious or moral convictions. The exemptions do not solve all problems; at times collaboration is not possible. In addition, there are voices in the US debate that see exemptions as violating the rights of others. Indeed, the first decade of this century has exhibited increased stress on the fabric of secular-sacred collaboration, especially for Catholic institutions. One case, inherited from the past century, was the Supreme Court decision of 1973 defining abortion as a constitutionally protected right for women. While the church and Catholic health care systems opposed the decision from the beginning, exemptions have been built into federal law providing conscience protections for individuals and institutions opposed to abortion.

But new, more recent challenges have emerged. Three issues beyond abortion illustrate how pluralism can test religious-moral convictions. In the social service network, adoption by gay parents became a test for Catholic Charities, which had been a leader in this field. In health care the Obama administration's contraceptive mandate for social services and other religiously based institutions became equally controversial. The controversy focused on the illegal requirement, at the outset, that religious agencies should provide insurance coverage for contraception. A looming concern is physician-assisted suicide laws, which have been enacted by several states and are being considered in several others; the possible consequences for the scores of Catholic facilities caring for an increasing elder population are not fully known. This chapter cannot probe these issues; nor is the intent to say that Catholic engagement on them has always been marked by an effective mix of principle and prudence. Indeed, in some instances it has not. It must be said that the legal struggle between the US Conference of Catholic Bishops and the Obama administration about the contraception mandate in the Affordable Care Act exhibited serious errors on both sides.

These issues arise from deep forces that will continue to shape the fabric of pluralism and social policy. While the pervasive popular support for religion still marks American pluralism, specific sectors of American society, namely, the academy and the law, have taken on a stronger secular tone. Meanwhile, independent forces, dynamic medical technology, and protections for the LGBTQ community in American law and policy combine with academic and legal themes to pose new questions for managing pluralism justly, fairly, and effectively. All this makes the intellectual and institutional challenge for Catholicism more complex but ever more necessary to engage. Engagement requires skillful interpretation and creative application of Catholic moral theology, bioethics, and social teaching.

The engagement, in my view, should not be undertaken primarily to protect ecclesial interests. The work of these Catholic social institutions is one way (surely not the only way) to continue the call of *Gaudium et Spes*. Hence both motivation for engagement and the explanation of it should be undertaken as a service to civil society and particularly to the poor, to families, to immigrants, and to children. There is clearly a need in the US system of social policy for the three dimensions of Catholic engagement: education, social service, and health care. Comparing the US system to other OECD countries, one could say that it expects less from the state, more from the market, and a great deal from nonprofits in responding to issues of poverty, socioeconomic justice, and adequate health care for all. The Catholic infrastructure, the mandate of *Gaudium et Spes*, and Catholic social teaching provide multiple reasons why Catholic institutions can be a significant resource for civil society.

The challenges to church-state collaboration can arise from legislative or executive mandates, from decisions of the courts and from the culture itself. Effective engagement with pluralism requires constant assessment within church structures about both emerging opportunities and emerging obstacles to collaboration. The tone of Catholic responses to both opportunity and obstacles should sustain the style of *Gaudium et Spes*. The church-state strategy should be realistic but not committed to gain maximum advantage in every conflict. Prudence has often been lacking at the national level of response to secular engagement. Not every fight must be engaged and not every compromise rejected. Catholic institutions today rightly invest heavily in maintaining "Catholic identity" even as they carry out secular functions in society. In this way they contribute to the common good of a religiously pluralist democracy with a secular state and a market economy. The record shows that it is possible to preserve Catholic identity in policies, practices, and professional behavior and also be a compassionate and competent contributor to the needs of society. Pluralism is here to stay in modern societies. Catholicism today should welcome it as a given and work with it intelligently and effectively.

NOTES

1. In the Marianist Award Lecture at the University of Dayton, Ohio, I used these three categories of Catholic teaching but developed them in a different way from the argument used in this chapter. See *The Church in the World: Responding to the Call of the Council* (Dayton, OH: University of Dayton, 1995).

2. Pope Francis has provided in *Laudato Si'* (*On Care for Our Common Home*) (Brooklyn, NY: Melville House, 2015) the most extensive contribution on environmental issues thus far in Catholic social teaching.

3. Vatican II, *Gaudium et Spes* 2. The translation of conciliar texts is provided in Austin Flannery, OP, ed., *Vatican Council II: Constitutions, Decrees, Declarations* (Northport, NY: Costello Publishing Company, 1996) (rev. ed., inclusive language). Subsequent citations of these text appear in the chapter in parentheses.

4. Pope Gelasius, "Letter to Emperor Anastasius," in *From Irenaeus to Grotus: A Sourcebook in Christian Political Thought 100–1625*, ed. Oliver O'Donovan and Joan Lockwood O'Donovan (Grand Rapids, MI: Eerdmans, 1999), 179.

5. The now standard reference for commentary on the conciliar texts is Herbert Vorgrimler, ed., *Commentary on the Documents of Vatican II*, 4 vols. (Montreal: Palm Publishers, 1968).

6. Flannery, *Vatican Council II*, for both texts: *Dignitatis Humanae; Gaudium et Spes*.

7. Examples of the public social engagement of the church in the postconciliar era can be found in Adrian Hasting, ed., *Modern Catholicism: Vatican II and After* (New York: Oxford University Press, 1991); Peter Nichols, *The Pope's Divisions: The Roman Catholic Church Today* (New York: Holt, Rinehart and Winston, 1981); John Eagleson and Philip Scharper, eds., *Puebla and Beyond* (Maryknoll, NY: Orbis Books, 1979); John A. Coleman, SJ, ed., *One Hundred Years of Catholic Social Thought: Celebration and Challenge* (Maryknoll, NY: Orbis Books, 1991). My piece in Coleman's volume analyzes, as this chapter does, the relationship of the conciliar texts *Dignitatis Humanae* and *Gaudium et Spes* ("The Right and Competence of the Church in the American Case," 55–71).

8. For an assessment of these themes from one of the major contributors to the text, see Pietro Pavan, "The Right to Religious Freedom in the Conciliar Declaration," in *Religious Freedom*, ed. Neophytos Edelby and Teodoro Jimenez-Urresti (Glen Rock, NJ: Paulist Press, 1966), 37–52; also Pietro Pavan, "Declaration on

Religious Freedom," in Vorgrimler, *Commentary on the Documents of Vatican II*, 4:49–86. My treatment is rooted in Pavan's commentary.

9. *Dignitatis Humanae* 7; John Courtney Murray, SJ, "The Problem of Religious Freedom," in *Religious Liberty: Catholic Struggles with Pluralism*, ed. J. Leon Hooper, SJ (Louisville, KY: Westminster/John Knox Press, 1993), 145.

10. *DH* 13: "The freedom of the Church is the fundamental principle governing relations between the Church and public authorities and the entire civil order."

11. For an examination of the development of Catholic thought on human rights, see David Hollenbach, SJ, *Claims in Conflict: Retrieving and Renewing the Catholic Human Rights Tradition* (New York: Paulist Press, 1979).

12. For the historical background of *Gaudium et Spes*, see Vorgrimler, *Commentary on the Documents of Vatican II*, vol. 5, which reviews the development and content of each chapter of the text.

13. Mark McGrath, "The Constitution on the Church in the Modern World," in *Vatican II: An Interfaith Appraisal*, ed. John H. Miller, CSC (Notre Dame, IN: University of Notre Dame Press, 1966), 397.

14. Yves Congar, *Lay People in the Church: A Study of the Theology of the Laity* (Westminster, MD: Newman Press, 1957), 78–102.

15. Murray, "The Issue of Church and State at Vatican II," in *Religious Liberty*, ed. J. Leon Hooper, SJ, 218–19.

16. Both the pontificates of John Paul II and Francis have addressed the modern world in terms drawn from *Gaudium et Spes* at times explicitly and at other times implicitly.

17. Both Pope John Paul II and Pope Benedict XVI built on the foundation of *Gaudium et Spes*. John Paul II's papacy, while conservative on internal policies, projected a ministry of justice and peace in teaching and practice. Benedict XVI, as a theologian at Vatican II, was critical of the evolution of *Gaudium et Spes*, but in his encyclical, *Deus Caritas Est* (2005), he wrote, "As the years went by and the Church spread further afield, the exercise of charity became established as one of her essential activities, along with the administration of the sacraments and the proclamation of the word: love for widows and orphans, prisoners and the sick and needy of every kind is as essential to her as the ministry of the sacraments and the preaching of the Gospel" (#22).

18. Murray's contribution to Catholic social thought was twofold: his detailed scholarly analysis of the church-state tradition, culminating in his major authorship of *Dignitatis Humanae*, extended over twenty years. The book *We Hold These Truths* addressed a range of specific issues in American society from a Catholic perspective. The description of pluralism offered at the outset of this chapter is drawn directly from him.

19. Two insightful accounts of Catholic participation in American public life are Peter Steinfels, *A People Adrift: The Crisis of the Roman Catholic Church in America* (New York: Simon and Schuster, 2003); and Charles R. Morris, *American Catholic: The Saints and Sinners Who Built America's Most Powerful Church* (New York: Times Books, 1997).

TWO

Against Pluralism

TERRY EAGLETON

My title, I suppose, is rather provocative—chin-leading, though not perhaps quite as challenging as, say, "The Evil of Nelson Mandela" or "Donald Trump and Hermeneutical Phenomenology." Its point is to remind us to be careful not to beg one or two questions—not to assume, for example, that the notion of pluralism is wholly unproblematic and then proceed to inquire in suitably humble spirit how the churches are to fit in with it. I take it that the Christian gospel is about critique rather than conformity and that such critique must be directed to the idea of pluralism as much as to anything else.

Let me begin, however, by speaking of plurality rather than pluralism. The claim that plurality is a good in itself is of course absurd. I mean, how many fascist parties do you want? There may seem something self-contradictory about having only one monopolies commission, but more might prove to be confusing. Much the same is true of diversity, a semi-sacred notion for postmodern thought. A prodigal range of gangland cultures is not to be encouraged. You cannot have more than one biological mother or pair of ears. The fact that you can't, however, is not a deficiency, let alone a tragedy. Having a well-nigh infinite supply of spouses is likely to throw up the odd problem from time to time. A diverse array of autocrats is not the most desirable of phenomena. The fact that the CIA has multiple forms of torture at its disposal is not to be commended. To claim that plurality and diversity are goods in themselves, to be always and everywhere preferred to singularity, is an emptily formalistic assertion, as well as a curiously universalizing one for those who tend to suspect that all universality is an ideological ploy. We need to know first the substance of these claims: What exactly is under discussion here? Are we speaking of a plurality of ethnic cultures or a plurality of methods of tax evasion? We need, in short, to be rather more pluralistic about the idea of plurality, as well as rather more diverse about the idea of diversity. Some forms of these things are supremely positive and some are thoroughly obnoxious—eighty-three fascist parties, for example.

Well, you might claim, plurality is not of course always and everywhere an inherent good, and certainly not when it comes to having three hundred different kinds of breakfast cereal; but it is, surely, when it comes to the social or political sphere. But this isn't true either. It was not difference and diversity that brought apartheid to its knees in South Africa, or that brought low the neo-Stalinist tyrannies in Eastern Europe. It was solidarity, a concept that most postmodern theorists treat with a certain wariness. Why? Well, largely because they tend to mistake it for some dreary uniformity. They find it hard to conceive of forms of human solidarity which don't simply flatten out difference. Yet not all forms of solidarity ride roughshod over the individual life. The Eucharist, for example. Or the Occupy movement. Solidarity and uniformity are not the same thing. They only look as though they are if you make a fetish of difference and diversity, and then treat whatever that challenges it as monochrome and authoritarian (people who do this, incidentally, are usually hostile to binary oppositions). For some pluralists, most forms of unity are "essentialist"—as though, incidentally, *anti*-essentialism is always on the side of the angels. But John Locke, father of bourgeois liberalism, was an essentialist of kinds, and Jeremy Bentham, founder of the dominant middle-class ideology of nineteenth-century England (Utilitarianism), was a positively card-carrying example of the species.

There are certain topics—whether we should bring back child factory labor in Manchester, for example—on which what we need is unity, not an exhilarating display of difference and diversity. When it comes to resisting the reintroduction of the death penalty or paying men and women equal wages, the more dreary uniformity we can muster, the better. It is unanimity we need on such questions, not plurality. An old English saying, one much admired by Ludwig Wittgenstein, declares that "it takes all kinds to make a world." Not always. There are some kinds we would be far better off without: racial supremacists, people with restless leg disorder who sit next to you on a flight from Sydney to London, Donald Trump, Simon Cowell, billionaire dictators with bank accounts in Switzerland, and countless others. The sooner such people cease to exist, the better, which is not to suggest taking a rifle to them.

No social system in history has been more hospitable to diversity, plurality, and heterogeneity than the capitalist marketplace, as Karl Marx recognized long ago. It's all about multiplying options. In fact, as one enthusiast for the market once observed, the future will be just like the present—only with more options. This may be his radiant eschatological vision, but it happens not to be mine. On the contrary—though this is another story—it seems to me that most of the important things are not a matter of choice at all. They choose you far more than you choose them. One does not choose to be born, or choose one's body, or choose to fall in love, or even choose to believe in God. The market is a positive riot of plurality, as the ideology of consumerism never ceases to insist. Nothing is more generously all-inclusive, more hostile to rankings, exclusions, hierarchies, and strict distinctions, than the commodity form, which in its typically promiscuous fashion will cuddle up to anyone at all as long as they have the money to buy it. So let us, as I say, be suitably pluralistic about the idea of pluralism rather than defend it in some absolute, monolithic, rigorously uncompromising spirit. Not all difference is to be celebrated—the distinction between beggars and billionaires, for example. The fact that you believe in welcoming immigrants, whereas I believe in trying to sink their boats with a few well-aimed rounds of gunfire, is not an invigorating instance of human diversity.

It is just the same with that other buzzword of our time, hybridity. The mixed, dappled, pied, impure, provisional, and indeterminate is considered intrinsically superior to the pure, singular, and definitive. But this is surely yet another false doctrine. The British National Health Service is becoming increasingly hybridized—which is to say, increasingly dominated by private medical provision—but that is not in my view to be commended. The US Republican Party is far from pure and singular, spanning as it does both liberals and Tea Party members, but I find myself churlishly refusing the suggestion that this all contributes to the rich variety of human existence. So, for that matter, does being struck by lightning, narrowly escaping drowning, and then falling down a manhole five minutes later. There's variety for you. As far as hybridity goes, there is no harm whatsoever in having a political organization made up of Theosophists, UFO buffs, Seventh-Day Adventists, and Prince Charles. It is just that it will never achieve anything.

Nor is there anything in the least objectionable in principle to exclusivity. Convicted pedophiles should be excluded from running children's holiday camps. Banning women from driving is deplorable, but shutting neo-Nazis out of the teaching profession is not. Postmodernist thought is keen on inclusivity but also, somewhat inconsistently, on marginality. It is good to be marginal but also good to be included, a position we can safely leave to the scrutiny of the logicians. The genuine pluralist, however, will want to distinguish between different forms of marginality, rather than monolithically embrace the concept in uncritical spirit. Neo-Nazis are marginal. Long may they remain so. Serial killers do not make up the majority of the population, unless a lot of people are being remarkably adept at covering up their crimes. In fact, there is nothing at all inherently positive about marginality, whatever the mindless mantras we are accustomed to hearing these days.

When it comes to pluralism in the sense of a multiplicity of beliefs, let us look very briefly at a common view of the situation. There are various peripheral groups in society who hold cultural beliefs very different from mainstream ones, and whose values and activities are of a minority kind. What we should do is afford them respect, celebrating their difference and otherness and refusing to insist that they conform to the dreary orthodoxies of the rest of us. One of these margins or minorities is known as Wall Street bankers. Now it may be that some of the culture that thrives among them—greed, naked self-interest, triggering an enormous economic crisis by the barefaced defrauding of others—is not quite in line with the dominant way of life of most of the population. It is not what most citizens get up to every day. Even so, who are we to criticize these people? Are not all human cultures to be valued? From what arrogantly Olympian position are we to pontificate that these men and women are "wrong"? Is not swindling other people, as the later Wittgenstein might say, just what they happen to do? Of course, other cultures must not foist their beliefs on us either. There are people who object to selling children into slavery, for example, which is fine as long as they do not keep hectoring the rest of us about it or keep insisting that their position is "right." After all, it would be a funny world if we all thought the same, as the old cliché has it. (After I had given this talk, a devout relativist in the audience insisted that she was opposed to ideas of right and wrong or truth and falsehood. She did not say which category she considered that statement itself to belong to, though the answer was clear enough.)

One of my oldest and dearest friends, the late Dominican theologian Herbert McCabe, was once giving a lecture critical of another theologian, who was sitting in the front row of the audience at the time. "I don't want to say," McCabe declared, "that the difference between me and him is one of emphasis. I want to say rather that I am right and he is wrong. Or, if he is right, then I am wrong." This is not the kind of thing that liberals and postmodernists want to hear. Surely if you have a divergence of viewpoints and social interests, you can still meet somewhere in the middle? Where, then, is the middle ground between racists and antiracists? Semi-racism, perhaps? Or between those who think that the pope is a pleasant enough fellow and those (some of them not light-years distant from where we are right now in Dublin) who regard him as the Antichrist? Not to be able to say that I am right and you are wrong may also mean not being able to say that you are right and I am wrong, a highly convenient position for me to adopt. The relativist is invulnerable to counterargument.

It does not follow from this case that one is free to hang one's adversary upside down from the ankles and beat him around the head. It has, in other words, absolutely nothing to do with the question of tolerance or intolerance. Tolerance and intolerance are forms of social practice, not in the first place a matter of conflicting viewpoints. To say that you are wrong is not to be intolerant. It may be mistaken, but that's a different matter. There may be plenty of room for dialogue, mutual persuasion, and the like. It is just that there are some conflicts that someone is going to have to win and someone is going to have to lose. In the United

States, either the Black Lives Matter movement wins out or antiblack police do. Either innocent men and women stop getting killed or they do not. You can't have it both ways, which is something else the liberal doesn't generally like to hear. For the liberal, all definitive statements sound like dogmatism. One of the most serious blunders of our age is the prejudice that conviction itself is incipiently dogmatic. Having a passionate opinion begins to seem rather fanatical in the laid-back climate of a postmodern world. One wonders what Martin Luther King Jr. would have made of it.

One does not tolerate that of which one approves. I myself do not tolerate the existence of Guinness, but I do tolerate the existence of Tom Cruise. The idea of tolerance *implies* antagonism. It is not in the first place an attitude of mind, as though one strives to be a little more sympathetic to cases one basically finds fairly repulsive. It is a matter of how one behaves in practice towards those who take up such positions. (In a similar way, love for the gospel is not a state of feeling but a social practice. If it were a state of feeling its paradigm would not be the love of strangers and enemies, which is hardly a cozy affair.) There will be no tolerance in the kingdom of God, which is not to say that there will be intolerance either. Tolerance doesn't mean trying to see something positive in one's adversaries by moderating one's views or seeking out some common ground, as though there might be something in Scientology after all. On the contrary, there is nothing whatsoever in Scientology, and saying so is not a matter of intolerance. (It may well be a matter of excluding its practitioners, as some countries have, on the grounds of the harm they can do, but it isn't a question of torturing them or locking them up.) Not to tolerate Sikhs means to oppress them, not to disagree with them. Genuine pluralism is not a question of endless open-mindedness. Absolute open-mindedness is not in any case possible for human beings, who are constituted as subjects by certain deep-seated, largely unconscious commitments and orientations. But even if it were possible, it would be a luxury only the socially privileged could afford. There are others less fortunate who need a reasonable degree of certainty about how things stand with them in order to be free and fulfilled. The traditional Christian teaching is that faith is a matter of certainty, which is only objectionable if you have an unduly scientistic view of certainty. You can be certain that you are in love, or that Schubert is a better songwriter than Bob Geldof.

Coexisting pluralistically with others doesn't mean trying to be less convinced about one's own beliefs.

There is a bogus kind of pluralism that holds that a point of view is to be respected simply because it is a point of view. One does not of course agree with those who hold that Jews are inferior beings, but one should respect their case even so, recognizing that they may well advance it with honesty and integrity. It is hard to think of a more pathetically disingenuous argument. Almost every vile viewpoint one can think of (including, incidentally, the idea that Nelson Mandela was evil, which is still the opinion of some right-wing South Africans) has been touted by somebody somewhere at some time or other. Before long, one ends up believing in everyone's position but one's own. To tolerate a case is not synonymous with respecting it. One can accept that there are other opinions around the place, and that they have a right to being expressed (perhaps within certain legal limits), while repudiating them as utterly odious and saying so as forcefully as possible—the opinion that the Holocaust never happened, for example. Denying the Holocaust is a moral obscenity, but one can still tolerate such nonsense in practice if one chooses to do so. I must say that I myself find legislation that outlaws such denial quite abhorrent. Far better to let people say what they think and then take them apart.

Nor does pluralism necessarily imply relativism. There are all kinds of subjects on which there is no one self-evidently correct view. The true pluralist, however, will recognize that there is difference and diversity here too—that two conflicting points of view may sometimes both be acceptable, and sometimes not. There can be legitimate disagreement over whether Bach is a finer composer than Beethoven but not over the question of whether Chicago is in Saudi Arabia or whether starving people to death is morally superior to feeding them.

One of the more disreputable reasons why pluralism is part of the dominant ideology of contemporary Western civilizations is that convictions in such a climate don't really matter all that much. It is not conviction that holds advanced capitalist societies together, as it is what holds the Lutheran church or the Boy Scout movement together. In fact, one of the most astonishing aspects of liberal modernity is that as long as you roll out of bed, go in to work, pay your taxes, and refrain from beating up too many police officers, you can believe pretty much what you like. Or at least you can believe anything that isn't likely to undermine this very framework of tolerance. Just imagine how extraordinary this would have seemed to most citizens of classical antiquity or of the Middle Ages. That this is so is of course in one sense an inestimable gain. It belongs with the precious achievements of liberal society, which include the fact that the Purity Police are less likely than they were to break down your bedroom door at 3 o'clock in the morning (though as mass surveillance grows more and more intensive, this is becoming less and less true). But it is also because belief is not really all that important anymore. Late capitalism is an intrinsically faithless form of life. The market doesn't really care very much whether you're a Buddhist or a Baptist as long as you buy the stuff it has to offer. Consumerism is wonderfully liberal hearted, all-inclusive, and open-minded.

You can contrast this situation with the earlier history of the same social order, when there was a positive glut of belief around: Reason, *Geist*, Science, Progress, Freedom, Humanity, and the like. When the middle classes are still getting themselves established, they need to tell themselves some fairly tall tales; once they have evolved beyond that probationary point, they can afford to go post-metaphysical, post-ideological, and even post-historical. There is not that much room for grand narratives or abstruse metaphysical speculation in the pragmatist, relativist, secularized, rationalized context of the West today, which is one reason why it is so ideologically vulnerable when confronted with radical Islam, which has no such qualms about the metaphysical or foundational. In fact, belief of any sizable kind is not only largely superfluous but actually undesirable. It is potentially divisive, which is not exactly convenient for the political state. If you happen to be a religious type, for example, it is preferable not to make too much of a fuss over it. As the English wit remarked, it is when religion begins to interfere with your everyday life that it's time to give it up. In this sense it is a bit like alcohol. Perhaps Jesus should have taken this advice to heart and saved himself a lot of trouble.

There is a sense, then, in which late capitalist society can buy its pluralism on the cheap, once belief itself becomes less vital to the conduct of everyday life than it once was. It is also true that no form of pluralism can be complete, in the sense that you have to agree to differ, a process that involves all kind of laws, institutions, practices, and regulations that are shared in common by different groups. Otherwise pluralism won't work.

One should also remember that pluralism is a *specific* form of life, and thus, so to speak, nonpluralistic in itself—in the sense, for example, that it cannot allow antipluralistic cultures to subvert its framework. The liberal state is officially neutral with regard to any specific body of belief. Like the most judicious of BBC commentators, it has absolutely no views of its own, other than the view that viewpoints that undermine its own viewpoint, that is to say, its stance of neutrality, should be opposed. But since this much-vaunted neutrality means that the state is as supremely indifferent to, say, socialism as it is to fascism and neofeudalism, it isn't neutral at all if you happen to be a left-winger. Its neutrality is itself the taking up of a position. It may be an admirable position in the eyes of many citizens, but it is a position nonetheless, and one should not seek to pretend otherwise.

Even so, we do indeed inhabit a genuinely pluralistic world in at least this sense—that though almost everyone agrees that roasting people slowly over fires is not the best way to greet them when they arrive at your house for dinner, we can't agree on why we agree on this, and no doubt never will. And this really would strike certain citizens of classical antiquity and the Middle Ages as utterly bizarre. It is not as though we agree on the fundamentals but diverge on the particulars but that we are not even in accord on the very deepest kind of questions. It is fortunate in this respect that it is the political state, not belief, that in the end holds our societies together, since otherwise they might well be in dire danger of falling apart. The drawback, however, is that political power is ultimately coercive, which is never the most effective way of keeping the show on the road. This is why power needs to bed itself down in something that is noncoercive—something that is more tangible, immediate, palpable, and existential than itself. And this is known as culture. Culture in the everyday, anthropological sense of the word is the place where power sediments and naturalizes itself. In fact, it is what men and women these days are prepared to kill for. Or die for. One can see, then, the dangers of an excessive pluralism from the point of view of the state—of a whole medley of cultures and subcultures existing cheek by jowl. If these forms of life interpret power, law, and authority differently enough, it will be hard to sustain the coherence and communality on which any complex modern civilization relies.

The Christian gospel is a relentlessly uncompromising affair. In fact, there are really only two major objections to what it preaches. The first is that if there is a God, he must be hopelessly in love with Donald Trump. This is so ludicrous a proposition that it is probably the best argument for atheism ever advanced. The second objection is that the gospel requires one to abandon one's family and possessions and face the near-certainty of a squalid death in the name of truth, friendship, and justice. Truth in its eyes is not in the end pluralistic and many-sided but a cutting sword that shears through domestic ties, turns parents against children, and sorts the sheep from the goats. Either you fed the hungry or you did not. As far as I can recall, Jesus doesn't say, "There are all kinds of ways, truths and lives, and I'm one of them." Difference and diversity—Jew, Gentile, man, woman, master, servant, and so on—are not as vital as our common humanity in Christ.

THREE

Hegemonic Liberalism
and the End of Pluralism

PATRICK J. DENEEN

The organizers of this volume began with a settled conclusion if the title of this book is to be credited: *The Church in Pluralist Society: Social and Political Roles.* Its premise is one that is widely shared by most contemporaries—namely, that we live in an age of pluralism, reflected, for instance, in the political philosopher John Rawls's largely unquestioned assertion that a basic condition of modernity is the ineradicable existence of the "fact of pluralism." This assumption has led some of our age's leading thinkers, including Rawls, to conclude that "the fact of pluralism" requires a set of political and social arrangements, forms, and institutions that allows at most for a modus vivendi—a way of "getting along"—in which liberal citizens bracket any substantive claims about the "good" in favor of public ordering based on neutral procedural norms. Such procedural arrangements, called "the right," in turn allow for various group and individual pursuits of varied notions of the Good, so long as those pursuits do not interfere with procedural norms, above all disrupting the endeavors of others.

Within this basic set of assumptions, contributors to this volume have been asked to consider the social and political roles of the church in pluralist society. This suggests at the outset the presumption that the primary consideration of "church" is the way it might contribute to a decent pluralist society primarily through constructive participation within the foundational presuppositions of the liberal order arising from the "fact of pluralism." Such contributions must necessarily fall within the basic demands outlined in liberal theory, meaning that the/a/any church's contributions are likely to be welcome and uncontroversial where there exists an "overlapping consensus." One such form that they might take is a church's commitments to "social justice," the primary form that various Christian denominations have adopted as their principal stated public purpose, in accord with basic commitments of the liberal order.

However, any activities and commitments of a church are ultimately subject to constraints, where any substantive claims about the Good might lie outside such an overlapping consensus, or worse still, where those commitments are thought to contradict notions of right by asserting some form of the Good—or in Rawls's language, a "comprehensive doctrine"—that cannot be justified in terms that are accessible by public reason. Thus, in modern liberal society, areas of Christian activity and commitment that conform to the broadly liberal modus vivendi are generally acceptable and even lauded—such as the above-stated concerns for social justice. Commitments that are regarded as lying outside the modus vivendi or even based on grounds that are irrational and beyond "public reason" are rejected as a matter of public policy, such as bans on abortion, birth control, or (increasingly) euthanasia. As Pierre Manent has written:

> The logic to which liberalism tends is to dismiss [the] moral content
> [of its Christian roots] and replace [the] "objective" morality, held
> as valid by the different Christian churches, by a formal morality
> of "reciprocity" or "respect" by all of the "individuality" of all. To
> choose a crucial illustration, it is impossible for a society claiming
> to be in the Christian tradition to admit that the right to abortion
> be written into law, and it is impossible for a liberal society to refuse
> members this right.[1]

This summary conclusion, at least, might be thought to be implied by the basic premise of this volume's title, beginning as it does with the acceptance of the fact of pluralism and the suggestion that a/any church plays various "roles" within that constellation of pluralities—that it is, at best, one expression of the multifarious plurality of modern society. This summary view maps onto the fuller understanding of the Catholic Church's relationship to modern liberal society articulated by John Courtney Murray, who suggested that liberal society had established "articles of peace" for a pluralist society in which the (for him, Catholic) church could operate freely as one player with distinctive "roles" in an open liberal polity.[2]

But this claim about the fact of pluralism in modernity seems at least one that is contestable as an empirical matter, and even as a philosophical assumption, and puts to the test one basic assumption implied in this volume's title. A host of empirical studies and data by certain measures suggest that society is becoming far *less* pluralistic and diverse, far more homogeneous and standardized. The forces of globalization, which entails economic, social, and political integration, have led to measurable declines in certain forms of pluralism, particularly cultural variety and diversity in those areas where advanced neoliberalism is ascendant. This force seems related as well to the "fact of secularization," which today renders the Western liberal democracies increasingly similar in at least one respect: they are divided less into a rich and diverse variety of religions than into, increasingly, and broadly speaking, populations that are more and more irreligious with a decreasing and embattled remnant of religious believers. Far from reflecting an intensification of religious diversity, these remnant believers tend increasingly to see themselves as sharing far more in common, in contrast to increasingly aggressive secular critics, than defined (as they might once have been) by differences of theology and tradition. Given these "facts" arising from various "processes"—social, economic, and political—it could just as easily be argued that Rawls was incorrect about the basic condition of liberal democracy. Less than a container of the fact of pluralism, liberalism, it could be contended, is most fundamentally a philosophy and increasingly an instantiated reality that purges real diversity and pluralism. In fact it could be contended that liberalism is enveloping the world in a globalized market-based, ideologically driven and mass-produced homogeneity that is masked by a largely superficial pluralism. Efforts to regularize religious institutions—"church"—within this liberal frame might be considered yet another effort to transform actual pluralism into its superficial liberal form.

Economic integration has brought various cultures into contact, increasing the overall experience of pluralism and diversity, but those very forces of economic integration have had the long-term effect of dissolving cultures and homogenizing people within the single market system as well as a political system that is increasingly integrated. Yet consumers regard the market as the source of diversity, producing a simulacrum of cultural diversity by transforming diversity into seemingly countless market choices, even as those choices are managed and normalized by a homogenizing market and deracinated consumers. Markets are especially adept at packaging various offerings of diverse cultures to a globalized market. Even the appearance of near-infinite choice shrouds what becomes a systematic homogenization that renders all places fungible and standardizes consumer choices.

A typical American supermarket today offers a dizzying array of ethnic food choices, for instance, but many products in such settings are produced by large corporate firms that have standardized and regularized what were originally an array of culturally diverse methods and forms of food preparation, with locally specific variations, often in a single format that comes to be the default norm within a homogenized food industry. Thus, for instance, various Chinese, Spanish, and Indian cuisines are rendered palatable to Western palates. While one might find a dizzying array of brands tendering different offerings of chop suey, refried beans, and tikka masala sauce, the food producers pursue production and marketing strategies that ensure that the seeming variety of foods will largely be identical everywhere they are offered and largely indistinguishable from competing brands produced by another firm. On the one hand, the rise of such sections in supermarkets can be accounted as proof of the fact of pluralism; on the other, its standardization by a national and increasingly international market reflects a tactic by which a plenitude of actual diversity is homogenized by both producer and consumer demands to satiate the lowest common denominator in an atmosphere of mass marketing and flattened taste.

Even in the various stores, whether owned by local entrepreneurs or absentee corporations, more often than not, the seemingly endless variety of choices that confront a consumer in fact masks what are often a small number of monolithic sources, as advanced market capitalism has shown itself to be far less about competition than new forms of monopoly that are carefully managed so as not to provoke a public or government backlash. Among the best and most eye-opening investigations of many modern market practices is provided by the independent scholar Barry Lynn in his 2011 book, *Cornered: The New Monopoly Capitalism*. Lynn describes the purchasing and retail power of single companies or small groups of companies over such disparate fields as eyeglasses, certain categories of pet food, washer-dryer sales, auto parts, many aspects of food processing, surfboards, and medical syringes. The same situation would almost certainly exist in the sacred beer market were it not for the peculiarities of local alcoholic beverage regulations. Lynn describes companies that swallow their rivals and then, with competitive pressure diminished, set about "destroying product variety and diversity."[3]

In a recent interview, Lynn described the monochromatic market in eyeglasses, largely imperceptible to us because of the apparent variety and diversity of products and shops.

> You decide you're going to go shopping for a new pair of eyeglasses, and you go into Lenscrafters. You say, I don't like the prices here. So you go down the road to a place called Pearl Vision, you say, no, no I'm going to go to a cheaper place. So you go to Target Optical, or maybe Sears Optical, or maybe you go to Macy's Optical. You go to Sunglass Hut. What you don't realize, because you're going to all these different branded stores, is that all these stores are all owned by Luxottica, an Italian eyewear Goliath.
>
> Then you say, OK, you've finally learned that all these outlets are controlled by one company. So then you go to an independent boutique around the corner. Well, the fact is that a whole bunch of the brands that are on the shelves at that store are manufactured by Luxottica, because Luxottica has become the dominant manufacturer as well as the dominant retailer. That means that they have the power, to a large degree, to control what the independent boutique does as well.
>
> So wherever you go, you think there's all this competition, you see all these different brands of glasses, all these different brands of retailers. And yet in the midst of the system is a single giant company manipulating everything and everyone to its own advantage.[4]

This micro-homogenization of products is mirrored in the macro-homogenization of markets themselves, in which a diversity of local markets are rendered identical through the process of standardization, regardless of the particular culture or history of various places. An apt description of such standardization appeared over a decade ago in an article in the *New York Times*, describing the transformation of a once-distinct, now largely standardized typical English downtown, Stratford-on-Avon.

> To survive the approach to the home where William Shakespeare was born, a striking timber-frame house in the center of this bustling town, it would be wise to bid adieu to all bucolic notions of quaint old England and ready oneself for the onslaught of globalization. A visitor must march past Country Casuals, Boots pharmacy, Next, and Marks & Spencer, and pass Accessorize, HMV, Whittard and of course, the dueling coffee shops, Starbucks and Costa Coffee. If it were not for Shakespeare's dwelling and a few notable old houses, this town—with row upon row of British chain stores—would scarcely be different from any other in Britain these days. Most butcher shops and hardware stores have closed. So have the family clothing shops, the fishmongers and a long list of other independent businesses. "If someone blindfolded you, put you in a helicopter and set you down in a town somewhere in England, you wouldn't be able to tell where you are anymore," said Jim Hyslop, 55, who lives just outside Stratford. The chain stores, he said, "change the character of a place."
>
> In the past five years, chain stores owned by corporations and out-of-town megastores similar to Wal-Mart (one of them, Asda, is, in fact, owned by Wal-Mart), have come to dominate many British towns and cities, creating a palpable sense of homogeneity from Kent all the way to Cumbria, and drawing striking parallels to America. Many of the main shopping thoroughfares, so-called "high streets," now traffic in sameness: ubiquitous cellphone shops (Orange, Vodafone, O2); the familiar coffee chains (Starbucks, Cafe Nero and Costa Coffee); the typical clothing stores (Gap, Next, Warehouse); and the cookie-cutter restaurants (Cafe Rouge, ASK, Pizza Express). Neighborhood greengrocers are also on the way out, replaced by chain mini-supermarkets, most notably Tesco, a company that has become one of the world's top retailers.

"In the case of Britain, and especially England, there is a huge sense of identity investment in the image of towns and cities, and the notion that this sort of bland, gradual effacement of character is taking place has taxed people at a deep level," said Andrew Simms, policy director for the New Economic Foundation, an independent economic research organization that published a report in August called "Clone Town Britain."[5]

The market, of course, is merely one venue, if a centrally important one, in which the patina of diversity masks a deeper uniformity and functions as a vital training ground that shapes a citizenry to embrace a superficial pluralism that shrouds an otherwise deeper and more comprehensive homogeneity. The focus of consumers, for instance, will be the remarkable variety of automobile choices, ranging from sedans to sport utility vehicles to pickups to vans, with nearly every possible choice of color and a dizzying array of accessories—while leaving altogether undisturbed the question of whether there is any real choice about owning an automobile, given the way that we have largely configured our spaces (especially suburban America).

We might extend the example from the marketplace to that of our main training centers that encourage the ideological embrace of liberal pluralism, namely, colleges and universities. Almost every college in America and increasingly the world now has various formal exercises to prepare students for a confrontation with "diversity," from orientations preceding the start of courses in their first year to programs and centers that sponsor a variety of programs on diversity to a growing embrace of curricular requirements in diversity training. The irony of the near-universal embrace of diversity training is lost on most campuses, which increasingly are generally indistinguishable in most respects, conforming to widespread academic norms that render most aspects of campus life effectively identical across most institutions. Faculty members are largely drawn from graduate programs that train future faculty according to standardized disciplinary norms. Administrators are almost wholly fungible, moving from institution to institution that may once have had distinctive religious and cultural features but are now eager to conform to a set of external as well as internalized norms that arise from standardized disciplines, bureaucratic groupthink, regularized accreditation agencies, and government regulation.

The diversity that is celebrated and embraced on college campuses is not unlike the purported diversity that is presented to the contemporary consumer. Superficially diverse—with an emphasis on race, ethnicity, sexual orientation, and the like—most students, faculty, and administrators reflect a narrow band of accepted beliefs and dispositions. Contemporary scholars of academic ideology such as Jonathan Haidt have written at length of the easily discernible group-think on many campuses today, claiming that what is extensively lacking on college campuses is diversity of ideas and beliefs, the central animating feature and even raison d'être of a university. "Universities are unlike other institutions in that they absolutely require that people challenge each other so that the truth can emerge from limited, biased, flawed individuals," Haidt writes. "If they lose intellectual diversity, or if they develop norms of 'safety' that trump challenge, they die. And this is what has been happening since the 1990s."[6] The *New York Times* columnist Nicholas Kristof penned a recent piece on this subject, calling for greater diversity of ideas and belief on campuses. The massive virulent and hostile reaction to his arguments by usually supportive readers was enough to prompt him to write a follow-up column pointing out the extent to which group-think had come to dominate leading institutions of contemporary society.[7]

If pluralism and diversity were the dominant trend of our society today, then we would see its evidence in a growing variety of human types, beliefs, and behaviors. We should see it perhaps above all in the universities, places that are purported hotbeds of pluralism and diversity. Yet students reflect the deeper homogenizing forces that shape most modern institutions and practices. They are educated usually according to norms required by college admission routines and expectations. In spite of claims of purported and widespread diversity, they are extensively homogeneous in terms of mass-cultural formation, which heavily rests on immersion in the internet and superficial "texting" and "snapchatting" that prizes irony, lack of seriousness, and lightly held commitments, as has been extensively documented by the social psychologist Sherrie Turkle in a number of studies, most notably her book *Alone Together*.[8]

In the place of cultural diversity, liberal orders celebrate "diversity" that is generally reducible to two forms: racial and ethnic variety and varying sexual identities. These forms of "diversity" map easily onto liberal homogeneity, and celebrated "differences" are almost universally undergirded by commonality of commitment to liberal autonomy and individualism within a universal and homogeneous liberal state. On campuses throughout America and around the world, students are taught that their primary responsibility is to respect and celebrate diversity, in effect requiring all students to embrace the same ethic of liberal toleration that trumps any actual cultural particularity or even "diversity." The program of preparing students to encounter extensive diversity in fact has the effect of a monolithic formation in lightly held indifferentism that is labeled toleration. Yet it does not have the virtue of toleration's original meaning, understanding actual and true differences. And despite the stress that leads to the possibility of fracture, this indifferentism "tolerates" those profound differences almost to the point of breaking. Modern forms of so-called toleration begin with a presumptive embrace and acceptance of diversity that calls for a preliminary commitment to shared indifference and that therefore renders contemporary liberal citizens into a monolithic group of like-minded believers in indifferentism. The only intolerance that can be tolerated is liberal hostility to deeply held belief that eschews this shared indifferentism, typically on the part of Christians or other orthodox religious believers, who now form a distinctive and increasingly marginalized minority group in acceptable liberal society.

Far from discerning evidence of growing diversity in rising generations—so-called millennials being the latest—empirical evidence from social science shows a discernible and very pronounced trajectory of human behavior and views that reflects ongoing and accelerating conformity to liberal norms. Those norms conform to deep liberal presuppositions about human nature, particularly anthropological individualism, a willingness and learned ability to enter and exit human relationships with frequency and ease without taking on deeply binding commitments, and a general consumer mentality that prefers a world of "optionality" to stability, commitment, and embeddedness. If we truly lived in a world of diversity and plurality, we would expect a certain randomness or unpredictability in certain measures of these features of contemporary human life, but instead we find a stark unidirectional march in a single and predictable direction, as reflected in a poll whose findings were released in 2014 by the Pew Foundation. The poll examined the beliefs and practices of four generations, born between 1928 and after 1980, and found a discernible and consistent trajectory that reflects the growing embrace of liberal belief and practice.[9]

As the poll demonstrates, the likelihood of millennials joining institutions such as political parties or religious institutions has waned in comparison to members of previous generations. Their likelihood of being married by the age of thirty-two has dropped precipitously in comparison to preceding generational cohorts, and their stated affiliation with nation, religion, and (surprisingly) even engagement with the environment demonstrates comparative declines. Moreover, as the data also demonstrate, these comparative declines in institutional affiliations and loyalties of various kinds can be tracked generationally, with strikingly uniform declines in affiliations from within each succeeding generation. As the liberal order becomes more fully instantiated, we see its formative power displayed in these various measures of "individualism" versus "membership."

Thus, contrary to the self-professed claims of the liberal order of neutrality about the Good in preference for generalized procedural norms that allow a flourishing of different conceptions and ideas and pursuits of the Good, the liberal order in fact shapes a people in keeping with a distinctive conception of human flourishing and bends people to a life in accordance with that vision, largely invisibly, although sometimes, and it seems increasingly, through power of law and backed by the threat of force. This formation is not happenstance or accidental but altogether a predictable and, indeed, promised outcome of the philosophical project of liberalism. While on the surface claiming to cure the problems of faction, division, and the fact of pluralism by allowing a flourishing of difference, in fact the foundational project of liberalism was to reshape the world to minimize and even eliminate the most elemental sources of pluralism and diversity—above all, culture and especially religion—and replace them with a pervasive and universal "anti-culture."[10]

Thus, as a matter of intellectual and philosophical honesty, the premise that liberal orders are neutral and "indifferent" to ends, or are even a form of the Good, should be discarded. Similarly, the claim that liberal orders encourage or defend "pluralism" and diversity should be treated with justified skepticism, joined to a willingness to perceive in those claims a deeper formative effort to shroud a pervasive homogeneous monoculture in a patina of variety. The fact that such shrouding has become so prevalent suggests at the very least the recognition that the homogenized monoculture of liberal orders is unappealing even to its proponents and requires obfuscation and even pervasive self-deception.

Liberalism was launched in particular in response to religious pluralism, with the claim that through state policies of neutrality toward
those beliefs and religious practices that did not negatively affect social
and political life, liberal orders would broadly tolerate a wide diversity of
religious beliefs and thereby encourage and result in extensive religious
pluralism. If this claim seemed to be justified in the early centuries of
liberal orders (especially in America), particularly given an explosion of
religious sects and beliefs within a society based on universal religious
toleration, the empirical evidence today suggests otherwise. Broad social
trends toward individualism, consumerism, and anti-institutionalism are
reflected in the declining membership in religious institutions, especially
among the young. The increase of "nones" as a growing percentage of
the population in America and Europe alike suggests that liberal orders
over time will have the effect not of encouraging pluralism, but a growing similarity of disposition and belief. Even among believers, the rise
of what the sociologist Christian Smith has termed "moral therapeutic
deism" provides further evidence that even internal religious belief will be
shaped by liberal norms of nonjudgmentalism, individualism, and relativism.[11] Indeed, one might compare with some profit the apparent pluralism of religious belief with the apparent pluralism of the marketplace.
While diverse on the surface, the market itself shapes a consumer mentality, shaping a people who value ease, comfort, and optionality. The same
arguably takes place as a result of the marketplace in religion.

Under liberal orders, a main feature becomes less its protection and
encouragement of religious diversity than a broader and increasingly universal view that religion is a private system of belief. Religion becomes
redefined as akin to a consumer product, an associational option among
the many identities one might choose. Belief itself increasingly becomes
seen within liberal society as a matter of private opinion, an otherwise
irrational set of beliefs that are harmless if maintained solely as a personal matter. A primary form of belief takes the place of religious belief—
whether one is religious or not—namely, that the obligatory first-order
belief is toleration of all religious belief. This first-order belief, in time,
demotes religious belief, even becoming a kind of new "religion" for
adherents of the liberal order. The insistence on the centrality of "diversity" and "pluralism" becomes monadic, brooking no dissent, especially
not from religious believers who might still insist that religious belief is

first-order. Those who are viewed as judgmental and intolerant are judged to be intolerable. Illiberal liberalism is an unsurprising outcome of liberal toleration.

Religion remains especially a matter of concern to liberal orders when it is manifested in an ongoing institutional form, laying claim by necessity to some portion of shared civic and even public life. Institutionalized religion is increasingly suspect as a potential opponent to the liberal order, and if it seeks to be an explicit participant in liberal society (not just an expression of "private" opinion), it must justify itself to liberal orders in terms that can be acceptable according to the tenets of "public reason." Thus we should be unsurprised by the challenge presented in this volume to consider the "social and political roles" of the church within liberal orders. To the extent that religious *institutions* can continue to gain cognizance and even esteem within liberal orders, they must justify their relevance and contributions in terms acceptable to the priorities of liberal orders.

In light of these claims, I want to conclude by discussing not any church but addressing distinct roles that might be played by the Catholic Church in particular. My suggestion is that the way forward is not to conceive these roles of the church *within* the liberal order but by presenting an alternative *to* the liberal order. This is to say that the Catholic Church should not accept its ascribed position, nor should it seek to gain acceptance within the liberal order, as one iteration of a privatized Good that enters the marketplace of superficial pluralism. Rather, it should robustly embrace its comprehensive alterity to the deepest presuppositions of the liberal order and self-confidently assert itself as an alternative to an otherwise homogenizing anti-culture. The church should not understand itself to be a corrective within the liberal order but a society in contrast to the liberal order, its deepest presuppositions constituting a fundamental alternative to liberalism's basic features that are increasingly instantiated in a pitiless global monoculture.

To outline very briefly the nature of the "contrast society" offered by the church, I would point to three broad areas of distinction. First, the church offers a profound vision and experience of relationality, in contrast to the anthropological individualism that lies at the heart of liberal orders. That fundamental relationality is manifest in the Trinity (the name of the university where this paper was first delivered), embedded in the most radical belief of Christianity of God Godself as a relationship with God-self and, further, all creation, in contrast to the vision of humans as related solely by utilitarian contract that lies at the heart of liberalism. Liberalism was inaugurated by positing a fictional "state of nature" comprising radically autonomous selves, but it has taken the transformation of the world in the image of this imaginary construct to bring this vision of humanity into being *in fact*. It is one of the hallmarks of our age that people have been *made into autonomous selves*, simultaneously through the engineering of the modern liberal state and the marketplace. This manufactured self required Promethean remaking of the world to dislocate people from hearth, home, family, community, and faith, and having achieved its end—as Alexis de Tocqueville predicted—humans are not now more empowered but rendered solitary, weak, lonesome, with only the raw marketplace and soft despotism of statist bureaucracy to turn to in times of need.

Second, both Christianity and liberalism envision humans as restless creatures—but the nature and object of that restlessness are profoundly different. The restlessness famously articulated by St. Augustine—"our hearts are restless until they rest in Thee"—is a restlessness that hopes for and anticipates final rest and satisfaction. The restlessness lying at the heart of liberal orders is insatiable, described in Hobbes's psychology as the creature driven by "power after power that ceaseth only in death." This restlessness was for Tocqueville one of the features that most distinguished the modern democratic person, which he described as the frenzied and ceaseless effort always to be finding something better, a ceaseless dissatisfaction with whatever worldly attainments achieved, the gnawing anxiety that one's status and reputation relied on constant competitive advantage of one's fellow citizens. Of these people he wrote in *Democracy in America*, they "are the freest and most enlightened people placed in the happiest circumstances the world affords, but it seemed to me as if a cloud habitually hung upon their brow, and I thought them serious and almost sad, even in their pleasures."[12] The restlessness of Augustine's longing translates not into the ceaseless dissatisfaction of the consumer or the anxiety of the status seeker but the steadiness and even joy of the pilgrim. To be a pilgrim is to journey with a destination, and that final destination is anticipated in many varied pilgrimages that remain destinations all around us—such as, on my campus of Notre Dame, the Grotto (a replica of the Grotto at Lourdes), or in Ireland, Croagh Patrick. Such destinations are not so much "bucket lists" as anticipation of the final satiation of our restlessness—pilgrims, not tourists.

Third, in contrast to liberalism's elimination of varied human pluralities achieved through its elimination of the preconditions of culture and the replacement of culture with a pervasive anti-culture, the Catholic Church not only presents a profound cultural inheritance as a rich vessel of human experience, but embraces the preconditions of culture that give rise to the extraordinary variety and true diversity and plurality that constitute the richness of Catholic culture. Those preconditions are threefold: time, place, and nature. The church together marks, keeps, and anticipates time, reflecting its embrace of the experience of time in its fullest horizon, linking the present to the past and the future, and thereby encouraging a deep and personal encounter with gratitude for an inheritance received and obligation for a gift to be stewarded. The church, while universal, is also profoundly local, rooted in places, beginning with the parish and radiating outward to diocese, sacred spaces near and far, and Rome as a simulacrum and promise of an Eternal city. And the church is the original Green movement, devoted to the ideal of sacramentality rooted in an understanding of the goodness of the created order, accompanied by a call to stewardship as a primary duty in humanity's relationship with the world. In all these respects, the church presents a profound alternative to liberal orders, which rest on reducing the human encounter with the past and future and residing instead in a pervasive presentism, which commends placelessness and deracination as the precondition of individual freedom and therefore by default cultivates a pervasive ignorance about, and lack of care for, our particular places; and which equates the achievement of individual autonomy through the domination and mastery of nature, which from its outset liberalism regarded as an obstacle to human liberation.

The church's role—if we can put it that way—is to forthrightly, confidently, and courageously understand that it is an alternative to the spirit of the age—in this age and all times—and not to be fitted into its prevailing tides. It can't merely be a corrective or a balm but, perhaps especially in our age, something wholly Other. In this respect, perhaps the church is, and can be understood to be, the persistence of a true pluralism in the midst of monolithic liberalism, although current trends would suggest that its decline in the West shows it is fundamentally subject to liberalism's homogenizing forces. More deeply, the church is a protector and guarantor of true pluralism, that pluralism of a single church so variously expressed through the ages into our own time. The dizzying array of architectural forms, the multifarious cultures that have arisen around the saints, the variety of religious orders such as those who sponsored the conference from which these chapters arose, the array of festivals and feasts, the rich and continuing legacy of art—sculpture, painting, music— all of which itself is the tiniest effort to approach in worship and wonder the plurality of God's unity, the many-ness of Christ, the many faces of Mary, the vast canopy of the witnesses. In our age of flattened earth, narrowed horizons, conformity to a shallow consumerism, and superficial variety that masks a deeper conformity, the role of the church is to be the church, and if it has the courage to be itself, that will be the greatest contribution that it can make to this or any age.

NOTES

1. Pierre Manent, "Michael Novak on Liberalism," in *Liberty/Liberté: The American and French Experiences*, ed. Joseph Klaits and Michael H. Haltzel (Washington, DC: Woodrow Wilson Center Press, 1991), 209. Manent goes on: "Instead of hoping for a reconciliation between the two traditions, perhaps we could limit ourselves to asking those who are more Christian than liberal not to make themselves unbearable to liberal opinion, and those who are more liberal than Christian not to render liberal society unbearable for religious people" (210).

2. John Courtney Murray, SJ, *We Hold These Truths* (New York: Sheed and Ward, 1960), 56, 78.

3. Barry Lynn, *Cornered: The New Market Capitalism and the Economics of Destruction* (New York: Wiley, 2011).

4. Lynn Stuart Parramore, "How the New Market Capitalism Will Crush You to Smithereens" (Interview with Barry Lynn), www.alternet.org/economy/how-new -monopoly-capitalism-will-crush-you-smithereens.

5. Lizette Alvarez, "To Be a 'Clone Town,' or Not: That Is the Question," *New York Times*, November 1, 2004, A4.

6. Jonathan Haidt, cited by Nicholas Kristof, "A Confession of Liberal Intolerance," *New York Times*, May 7, 2016, www.nytimes.com/2016/05/08/opinion/sunday /a-confession-of-liberal-intolerance.html.

7. Kristof, "A Confession of Liberal Intolerance." See also "The Dangers of Echo Chambers on Campus," *New York Times*, December 10, 2016, www.nytimes .com/2016/12/10/opinion/sunday/the-dangers-of-echo-chambers-on-campus .html.

8. Sherry Turkle, *Alone Together: Why We Expect More from Technology and Less from Each Other* (New York: Basic Books, 2012).

9. See "Millennials in Adulthood," Pew Research Center, www.pewsocial trends.org/2014/03/07/millennials-in-adulthood/.

10. I discuss the growth of a liberal "anti-culture" in my book, *Why Liberalism Failed* (New Haven, CT: Yale University Press, 2018), ch. 3.

11. Christian Smith and Melinda Lundquist Denton, *Soul Searching: The Religious and Spiritual Lives of American Teenagers* (New York: Oxford University Press, 2009).

12. Alexis de Tocqueville, *Democracy in America*, trans. George Lawrence (New York: Harper Perennial, 1969), II.i.,13, 536.

FOUR

The Church in a World of Options

HANS JOAS

A lack of public attention is not what the Catholic Church should currently complain about. Unfortunately, not all that attention is benevolent, and despite the overwhelmingly positive reactions to the personal style and first pronouncements of Pope Francis in the media worldwide, we Catholics have good reasons to remain cautious. We are all familiar with the sudden reversals in popularity many public figures have experienced. Shortly before the resignation of Pope Benedict XVI there was talk of a very serious crisis of the church. Some even used the sexual abuse scandals, indications of corruption in the church, and a widespread feeling of institutional stagnation to claim that the church is at least approaching its most profound crisis since the Reformation. This should not be taken literally. From my—German—perspective, other phases in history like the secularization of 1803, Bismarck's attempts to suppress the Catholic Church in the 1870s, the rule of Nazism in 1933–45 and of communism in one part of Germany until 1989, and, of course, the far-reaching alienation between the church and the liberal bourgeoisie or the social democratic labor movement in the nineteenth and twentieth centuries deserve the label "crisis" more and make us hesitate to accept exaggerations. Others, from Mexico to China, will refer to their own histories in a similar way. Nevertheless, there can be no doubt that we are indeed in a situation in which a serious new reflection on the church is needed.

This new reflection has to be both theological and social-scientific. As we all know, the cooperation of theologians and social scientists has not always been easy; the social sciences are not regularly part of the educational profile of churchmen and churchwomen, and many theologians remain skeptical because they see the social sciences as driven by secularizing views and impulses. In that sense they may still find plausible the way Leo Tolstoy put it in a satirical piece of 1903, "The Restoration of Hell." There we hear a devil in hell boasting of having invented the new discipline of sociology to draw people away from the teachings of Jesus: "I impress on them . . . that all religious teaching, including the teaching of Jesus, is an error and a superstition, and that they can ascertain how they ought to live from the science I have devised for them called sociology, which consists in studying how former people lived badly."[1] Others, like José Casanova,[2] have already demonstrated that sociology can play a fruitful role in the debates of the church, and I hope that I can add further aspects to the picture.

Many people today certainly share an enthusiasm for certain documents of the Second Vatican Council concerning the selfunderstanding of the church in the contemporary world, from *Lumen Gentium* to *Gaudium et Spes*, including *Dignitatis Humanae* and *Nostra Aetate*. But when we refer to these documents today, half a century after the time when they were drafted, we cannot evade answering the question of why the reality of the church today differs to a large extent from what was articulated and promised in these documents. Our enthusiasm for the council may be an expression of our desperation about much of what happened since, and as social scientists, we have to develop an explanation for the discrepancies between the spirit of the council and the hard realities of the church or the world in which it finds itself. One possible explanation is that the council itself failed to translate its vision of the church into a clear and feasible program of institutional reform. The sociology of organizations teaches us, however, that institutional structures and their inertia easily resist lofty declarations and tend to restabilize themselves after phases of turmoil or even roll back on what came up in such an exceptional phase. This explanation receives support from one of the best sociological studies on Vatican II, which describes the council as a process in which unexpectedly a kind of "collective effervescence" (Durkheim) set in, a creative and shared enthusiasm of the assembly, theologically interpreted as the operating of the Holy Spirit.[3] The documents are the products of this process, but the defeated minority did not necessarily give up its resistance to them after the council. A more radical explanation sees the documents themselves as not completely unambiguous. Not only their theological and philosophical vocabulary but also the visions of the church and the views of the "secular" world would themselves have to be clarified today. Given the fact that the council was indeed a process with unexpected results, it would be surprising if there were no inconsistencies and vague passages in these texts. Moreover, the strong pressure to present new things not as new but as being in continuity with the tradition of the church and to avoid the impression of rupture with, for example, the highly centralized, hierarchical, and dogmatically antimodern church of the nineteenth century made it very difficult for the council to become a guideline for later developments. The empirical fact that there has always been an interaction between moral developments and the teachings of the church—an interaction, not a determination in only one direction—still has to be recognized and respected in the self-understanding of a church that is willing to learn from the world.

A double movement is necessary. We have to be more specific and explicit with regard to the social-scientific understanding of the church and the contemporary world, on the one hand; on the other hand, we have to go back to the characterization of the church in the early statements of the Christian faith as we find it in the Nicene Creed, for example. These early characterizations had four dimensions: the church was declared to be "una sancta catholica et apostolica." By calling itself "one," long before humankind developed geographically correct knowledge of the globe and a full understanding of the varieties of civilizations and political orders in the world, the church developed a vision of all human beings brought together in one spirit. As, for example, the German cardinal Karl Lehmann has written, this unity is not only a vision, but always already a reality when, despite all real and potential divisions, Jesus Christ remains the common point of orientation for all Christians wherever and however they live.[4] Such unity should, however, not be misunderstood as uniformity; on the contrary, pressures toward uniformity will necessarily endanger unity.

Sanctity or "holiness" of the church does not mean that the church is an institution that is released from the human condition of sinfulness. And this is true not only for individuals but also for the institution itself. All members of the clergy, including the pope, are sinners, and while the church is, or should be, an attempt to realize on earth what can never be fully realized here, sacredness remains an inspiration and a normative yardstick, but it must not be turned into self-sacralization. Self-sacralization is a constant danger of all human institutions, and the idea of a "raison d'église" in analogy to the "raison d'état" prevents the institution from judging itself by the same high standards it uses with regard to others. Instead of being triumphalist, the church has to remain humble if it takes its mission seriously.

"Una sancta *catholica* et *apostolica*": The Catholicity of the church emphasizes its attempt to liberate itself from all cultural and national particularities, although not in the direction of a rational universalism but in the sense of a deep respect for cultural diversity coupled with an emphasis on the penetration of all cultures by the Christian message of salvation. A universalism that is not disconnected from the inherent particularity of all culture: that could be a contemporary paraphrase of what "catholic" intends to mean.

Finally, the "apostolic" character of the church, although referring to the apostles of Jesus Christ, is, above all, a call to continue the mission. It is the counternotion to a self-referential church, the emphasis on a goal outside that lies not in a transcendent dimension alone but in the human beings of the world.

A church that is missionary, nontriumphalist in its self-image and historical views, and aims at a concrete universalism: that is in my eyes the lesson that can be drawn from such a renewed reflection on the early statements of our faith. This must serve as the normative yardstick for our sociological analysis of the role of the church in the world and of its institutional structures. In the following pages I very briefly point to a few main features of what I consider a relevant sociological diagnosis of our time and then draw a few conclusions from such an analysis for what Christians and the church have to take into account in our time.

The crucial term in my analysis of the contemporary situation is "option." I rely on two great religious thinkers when I make that claim, namely, Charles Taylor and William James. The main accomplishment of Charles Taylor's monumental work *A Secular Age* is to have studied the rise of a so-called secular option, chiefly in the eighteenth century, in light of its prehistory, enforcement, and impact.[5] Taylor makes it clear that the rise of this secular option entails a fundamental shift in the preconditions for faith. Ever since this shift, believers have had to justify their particular faith, such as the Christian faith, not just as a specific confession or with respect to other religions but also as such, as faith per se—vis-à-vis a lack of faith that was initially legitimized as a possibility and then, as I argue with regard to some countries and milieux, even "normalized." Of course, the rise of the secular option as such should not be understood as the cause of secularization, but it does establish it as a possibility. In the first instance, then, the optionality of faith arises from the fact that it has in principle become possible not to believe. Subsequently, under the conditions of religious pluralism, this optionality has become even stronger. But here we need conceptual distinctions originally introduced by William James in his influential article "The Will to Believe." Options, James said, "may be of several kinds. They may be: 1. living or dead; 2. forced or avoidable; 3. momentous or trivial; and for our purposes we may call an option a *genuine* option when it is of the forced, living, and momentous kind."[6] I restrict myself here to the first element of this definition of a genuine option. "A living option is one in which hypotheses are live ones. If I say to you: 'Be a theosophist or a Mohammedan,' it is probably a dead option, because for you neither hypothesis is likely to be alive. But if I say: 'Be an agnostic or be a Christian,' it is otherwise: trained as you are, each hypothesis makes some appeal, however small, to your belief."[7] This distinction seems to me to be extremely relevant for the understanding of what one may call "genuine pluralism." If, as in many European societies, a Muslim minority lives together with a Christian or agnostic majority, where the majority does not feel attracted to Islam, nor the minority to the religious or secular views of the majority, this would then not be genuine pluralism. There were many such cases of a mere coexistence of different faiths in the past, and such a mere coexistence of a plurality of faiths would have to be distinguished from a genuine pluralism in which people of one orientation can indeed at least imagine to be attracted by a competing worldview. The precise extent to which faith has indeed become an option in this sense in different countries or milieus is, of course, an empirical question. But I think it safe to say that in contemporary Europe most Christian believers are constantly confronted with the option of a secular worldview and, moreover, that in the traditionally biconfessional societies of central Europe we can observe not only a shrinking of confessional milieus but also indications of an emergent transconfessional Christian milieu. The institutional differences between the Christian churches are no longer mirrored in the division of families, friendship networks, and sociocultural milieus. It is noteworthy that there are comparable developments in the United States.[8] Individuals are paying less and less attention to theological differences, particularly between the different forms of Protestantism, while individuals' political and moral affinities with particular religious communities are proving decisive to their appeal.[9] The majority of new marriages today are interfaith.[10] The religious landscape of the United States is constantly changing as a result of the emergence of new Christian churches that cannot be assigned to any major historical denomination.

But the significance of "optionality" is not restricted to the religious field. There are numerous sociological analyses of how people in "Western" societies experience the optionality of their most important social relations—friendship, love, family—but also, for example, of their professional careers or political affiliations. I cannot go into any detail here. Suffice it to say that this observable increase in options may lead to a situation where people are stretched to the breaking point. Crises of orientation, enduring confusion, and indignation may stunt the capacity for judgment or even lead to the aggressive elimination of options.[11] This is not a necessary consequence, though. We are all familiar with contingency-adapted forms of commitment, for example, to lovers and children. When fixed gender and generational roles are dissolved, behavioral insecurity may occur, but it is also possible that partners change the ways they interact with one another and their children. As early as 1945 the Chicago sociologist Ernest Burgess tried to capture this change when he referred to a shift "from institution to companionship."[12] In this process, the effort involved in coordination and discussion has to increase, and individuals have to become more sensitive to the nature of a given situation and to others' needs. These abilities compensate for the loss of "static" stability and potentially generate a more elevated, "dynamic" form of stability.

We are living today, therefore, in a world of options. But this is true in another sense as well, not only with regard to the great number of options we encounter in the world, but also with regard to the ever more intense process of globalization. Perhaps the most important sociological trend regarding Christianity today is the enormous globalization of Christianity itself. Serious observers, like Philip Jenkins,[13] speak of our time not as an age of secularization but as one of the most intense phases of the expansion of Christianity in history. This expansion partly has demographic reasons (rapid growth of the population in some Christian countries), but that is not the whole story. There are also some impressive success stories of mass conversion to Christianity in Africa, as well as in South Korea and parts of China. Through migration and a fundamental shift in the geography of power outside and within the churches this will rather sooner than later affect Christians in Europe and North America in many ways.

All these processes that can be described by historians and sociologists of religion have enormous intellectual, for example, theological, implications. One of the first thinkers to realize this was Karl Rahner. In a retrospective article on Vatican II originally published in 1979, the great theologian who had been deeply involved in the drafting of the council documents already recognized that the council constituted a "qualitative leap," as he said, for the Catholic Church on its way to truly becoming a world church.[14] What it has always been *in potentia*, it is now becoming *in actu*, he wrote. One of the reasons the council led to the experience of collective effervescence clearly seems to have been the intensity of the mutual encounter of bishops and theologians from all over the world. Rahner saw this as the beginning—and not more than the beginning—of a totally new phase in the history of the church, comparable for him only to the "radical new creation" of St. Paul when he transcended the limitations of a Jewish religious sect and turned Christianity into a magnet for people from the whole Mediterranean world of his time. More than even Rahner might have anticipated, this leads to a new constellation of "genuine pluralism" in large parts of the world. Christianity is becoming a living option for people for whom it was either not available before or tainted by the missionary activities of colonial powers.

But for the Christians in Asia the long intellectual and religious traditions of their own civilizations also remain living options. In the words
of the Cambridge church historian David Thompson, "Asian Christians
have therefore sought to understand all world faiths as being in some
way vehicles of God's self-revelation: in this respect they asked questions
similar to those asked by western missionaries. Almost inevitably this has
raised questions about Christology. . . . Comparisons between Jesus and
Krishna or Buddha seem to require abandonment of any Christian claim
that God is uniquely revealed in Jesus Christ. This in turn raises the question of whether Christianity was distorted as it was expressed in Hellenic
culture."[15] While these questions are not new, they are now posed in non-
European contexts in new and challenging ways.

The two main new constellations of optionality I have briefly sketched
here—the confrontation of the Christian faith with widespread irreligion
in Europe and a few other countries outside Europe and with Asian and
African cultural traditions on other continents—have a striking similarity.
They both undermine the fusion of the Christian faith with particular
European cultural traditions. I am deeply interested in investigating what
this means for a contemporary rearticulation of the Christian faith. All
theologies that do not take seriously these challenges seem to me obsolete.
But I will not go into these intellectual challenges for Christianity here.[16]
They certainly force us to speak in a new language, not in the linguistic
sense, of course, but in ways that are based on distancing oneself from a
traditional idiom and permeated with an understanding of other civilizations and of the achievements of secular worldviews. They also force us to
"elementarize" the faith, as the East German bishop Joachim Wanke put
it, to take the hierarchies of truth in the Christian faith very seriously.[17]

Instead of elaborating these intellectual challenges for contemporary
Christianity, I conclude with a short sociological reflection on the Catholic
Church as an institutional structure. In the course of the second half of the
nineteenth century, mostly Protestant church historians began to integrate
insights from the emergent discipline of sociology in their research, and
around 1900 some of the greatest figures in sociology began to investigate
which forms of social organization were created out of the spirit of religious
innovations. Max Weber distinguished between two main types of religious organization in Christianity, the church and the sect; his friend and
rival Ernst Troeltsch introduced a third form called mysticism or individual

spirituality. They did not consider the types they described as exclusive. When discussing the Salvation Army, for example, Troeltsch clearly was sensitive to further types—the army as model for a religious organization. There are four reasons that these attempts are relevant for the contemporary situation in which we discuss the possibilities for a renewal of the Catholic Church "in a secular age." The first reason is that the typology of Christian churches and groups here is not simply an attempt to develop a classification. It is much more ambitious, namely, an attempt to study institutions by putting them back into their *status nascendi*. We should not take the existence of the church for granted but recognize how improbable its emergence and growth were. The second reason is that these sociologists of religion took the plurality of Christian religious organizations seriously, and this in a value-free manner. They did not treat sects or the formation of spiritual communities as aberrations from the path of the only saving church, nor did they, like the sectarian tradition, condemn the church as necessarily corrupt, decadent, authoritarian, or whatever. All these organizations have, according to Troeltsch, their own "sociological logic." This also implies that they denied (my third reason) a historical teleology in the direction of one of these main types. They do not assume that the church will definitely defeat the stricter organizations based on voluntary membership ("sects") or the tendencies toward religious individualization,[18] but they see an interplay of these organizations, new developments in one direction as reactions against developments in the other direction, and individual biographical trajectories leading through different types of Christian religious organizations. And, my fourth reason, Max Weber and in our time Robert Bellah open our eyes to the parallels between the emergence of the Christian church and the institutional innovations brought about by the other religions based on the innovations of the "axial age." All these religions have a certain potential for a utopian order that they preserve in special types of institutions, "relaxed fields within the 'gentle violence' of established social orders and sometimes the not so gentle violence in times of political turmoil."[19] In India, the tradition was carried by the hereditary caste of the Brahmins, while the Buddhists invented monasticism and the ancient Greeks and Chinese developed philosophical schools. The dialogue between such a historical-sociological analysis of the church or of the history of Christianity in general with the theological self-interpretation of the church seems to me to be a pressing task in this "world of options."

This task is all the more pressing since a number of easily available interpretive patterns of the church have lost their plausibility. The church cannot simply become a membership organization, nor should it be imagined as a quasi-state. Charles Taylor has taken up ideas from Henri de Lubac and Yves Congar and spoken of the church as—at least potentially—a "network of agape." I agree that the ethos of love has to be the guiding idea and that the idea of a network could be attractive as an antidote to the hierarchical centralization of a quasi-state. But perhaps the most fruitful idea so far is the idea of a synthesis of the main types of social organization from the history of Christianity. We have to preserve the universalism of the church but integrate into it the pluralism of the voluntary organization that energizes the sects. And this renewed church ought to be experienced by the individual believers, not as an impediment for individual spiritual development as it unfortunately often is, but as enabling such development. That at least was the perspective of Ernst Troeltsch with whose characterization of Catholicism I would like to conclude.

> Catholicism is not the miracle of rigid consistency which it has
> often been considered. From its beginning on it has been an
> infinitely complicated system full of contradictions that has again
> and again in ever new ways attempted to combine fantastic popular
> religion and philosophical dogma, revolutionary individualism and
> absolute authority, profane cultural techniques and otherworldly
> asceticism, lively laymanship and priestly domination—a
> masterpiece of mediation that created in church authority only the
> ultimate regulator for the cases in which these mediations lead to
> frictions and a lack of clarity.[20]

NOTES

This essay was originally published in Joao Vila-Cha, ed., *Renewing the Church in a Secular Age: Holistic Dialogue and Kenotic Vision* (Washington, DC: Council for Research in Values and Philosophy, 2016), 85–96, and is reproduced here with the permission of the publishers.

1. Leo Tolstoy, "The Restoration of Hell," in *On Life and Essays on Religion* (Oxford: Oxford University Press, 1934), 309–30, at 326.

2. José Casanova, "A Catholic Church in a Global Secular World," in *Renewing the Church in a Secular Age: Holistic Dialogue and Kenotic Vision*, ed. Charles Taylor et al. (Washington, DC: Council for Research in Values and Philosophy, 2016), 67–84.

3. Melissa J. Wilde, *Vatican II: A Sociological Analysis of Religious Change* (Princeton, NJ: Princeton University Press, 2007).

4. Cardinal Karl Lehmann, "Catholic Christianity," in *Secularization and the World Religions*, ed. Hans Joas and Klaus Wiegandt (Liverpool: Liverpool University Press, 2009), 23–45, at 26–30.

5. Charles Taylor, *A Secular Age* (Cambridge, MA: Harvard University Press, 2007).

6. William James, *The Will to Believe* (New York, 1905), 1–31, at 3; original emphasis.

7. Ibid.

8. See Hans Joas, *Faith as an Option: Possible Futures for Christianity* (Stanford, CA: Stanford University Press, 2014), 116–25.

9. Robert Wuthnow, *The Restructuring of American Religion* (Princeton, NJ: Princeton University Press, 1988).

10. Robert Putnam and David Campbell, *American Grace: How Religion Divides and Unites Us* (New York: Simon and Schuster, 2010).

11. See Joas, *Faith as an Option*, 78–91.

12. Ernest W. Burgess, *The Family: From Institution to Companionship* (New York: American Book Company, 1945).

13. Philip Jenkins, *The Next Christendom: The Coming of Global Christianity* (Oxford: Oxford University Press, 2004).

14. Karl Rahner, "Theologische Grundinterpretation des II. Vatikanischen Konzils," in *Schriften zur Theologie*, Bd. XIV (Köln, 1980), 287–302.

15. David M. Thompson, "Introduction: Mapping Asian Christianity in the Context of World Christianity," in *Christian Theology in Asia*, ed. Sebastian C.H. Kim (Cambridge: Cambridge University Press, 2008), 3–21, at 13–14.

16. Joas, *Faith as an Option*, 126–38.

17. Bischof Joachim Wanke, "Wie heute von Gott sprechen, . . . im nichtchristlichen Umfeld," Vortrag, Munich, St. Bonifaz, 27 March 2012 (unpublished manuscript).

18. Ernst Troeltsch, *Die Soziallehren der christlichen Kirchen und Gruppen* (Tübingen: Mohr Siebeck, 1912). The interesting book by Rainer Bucher suffers from the tendency to connect organizational types and historical phases too closely. See Rainer Bucher, . . . *wenn nichts bleibt, wie es war: Zur prekären Zukunft der katholischen Kirche* (Würzburg: Echter, 2012).

19. Robert N. Bellah, *Religion in Human Evolution: From the Paleolithic to the Axial Age* (Cambridge, MA: Cambridge University Press, 2011), 596.

20. Ernst Troeltsch, "Modernismus," *Die Neue Rundschau* 2 (1909): 456–81. Here quoted after Troeltsch, *Gesammelte Schriften II* (Tübingen, 1913), 52–53. (abbreviated translation by the author).

FIVE

The Church's Place in
a Consumer Society

The Hegemony of Optionality

WILLIAM T. CAVANAUGH

In the first year of the new millennium, the journalist Tom McGurk wrote:

> We have reached a nemesis in our affairs in Ireland where
> consumerism is in the process of replacing Christianity as the
> shaping influence on all our lives. We are rapidly approaching a
> point where the social and moral order is being dictated by market
> forces alone. As we build shopping centres with the zest that we
> once built cathedrals and as brand names replace saints' names, the
> land of saints and scholars is being recast as the land of customers
> and consumers.... There is a sense out there that the whole business
> is out of control.... There is no longer any national consensus about

what we want as a society, merely a bunch of politicians making it up as they go along.[1]

McGurk is certainly not alone in his lament about Ireland; in 1978, for example, a statement released by the National Conference of Priests of Ireland had complained, "We feel that the swamping of Ireland by consumerism has created an environment hostile to the survival of real religion."[2] Ireland is certainly not unique in exhibiting the waxing of consumerism and the waning of the church. The sense that something dear has been lost in the process is a sentiment shared by many Christians in Ireland and in the West more generally.

McGurk identified an important problem that the church must face directly, but the problem needs careful examination if the church is not simply to fall into resentfulness and nostalgia. It will not do to appeal to a past age of "national consensus," presided over by the church. In the rhetorical battle of consensus versus pluralism, consensus will lose every time. Who would want to return to an age of conformity when we have more choices today than ever before? More choice equals more freedom, and freedom is seen as an unqualified good, even if people sometimes use that freedom badly, in the mad pursuit of material gain, for example. It can be persuasive to question the choices that people make; in the current cultural context, however, it is virtually never persuasive to question the value of choice itself.

Nevertheless, it is at that deeper level of the underlying conditions of choice itself that we need to understand the current situation. It is hyperbole to say that Ireland has jettisoned Christianity in favor of consumerism. It is more accurate to speak of the changes in Irish society in terms of Charles Taylor's concept of optionality. For Taylor, secularization is not simply a change in what people believe but in the underlying conditions of belief. A great many people in Ireland and in the West more generally still believe in God and many still go to church. What has changed most profoundly is the fact that belief in God and participation in the church is now optional in a way that it was not before. It is not much of an exaggeration to say that in 1950 to be Irish was to be Catholic; this is no longer the case. Catholicism is now optional in Ireland in a way that it was not in the not so distant past. Taylor's task in his massive book *A Secular Age* is to explain this process for the modern West.

He writes, "The change I want to define and trace is one which takes us from a society in which it was virtually impossible not to believe in God, to one in which faith, even for the staunchest believer, is one human possibility among others."[3]

Taylor acknowledges that optionality poses challenges for many believers who find it hard to hold onto their faith under such conditions, but he thinks that optionality is simply the world in which we live now and that the condition is irreversible; he refuses nostalgia and thinks that there are advantages for believers, like himself, in such a world as opposed to one in which conformity was forced. Many people go much further and narrate the move to optionality as an unqualified gain: who wants only one choice when one can have many choices? The move to optionality in Irish society is often narrated as liberation from narrow conformism to a healthy pluralism. There is now more than one way to be Irish, and we should celebrate the blooming of myriad new choices.

The paradox of optionality, however, is that optionality is not optional. If optionality has become the new consensus, then it is not a simple matter of contrasting consensus with optionality or pluralism. What happens when optionality becomes hegemonic? This chapter explores this theme, which lurks as a kind of "unthought" in Taylor's work. It links optionality to the phenomenon of consumerism, a theme underexplored in Taylor's work, and argues that to embrace consumerism is not necessarily to move to a pluralistic society. The way that Ireland's confrontation with modernity has been narrated is discussed first. Next Taylor's analysis of optionality is examined. The chapter then explores the ways that conformity and nonconformity interact in consumer society, followed by an examination of how power is exercised in and by a society of optionality. Finally, the theme of consumerism as religion is explored, and some suggestions are made for how the church might respond.

IRELAND AND MODERNITY

Ireland is an example of what has been called "compressed modernity," because economic modernization and secularization have followed a path similar to those of other Western countries but at a much faster rate.[4] Ireland is sometimes compared to Quebec, where the hegemonic position of the Catholic Church collapsed seemingly overnight in the Quiet Revolution of the 1960s.[5] The term "compressed modernity" is also used to refer to rapid economic and social change in South Korea since the 1980s, though the Catholic Church there has grown by 70 percent since the year 2000; over 10 percent of the total population of South Korea is Catholic, and that number continues to grow. South Korea has had more Catholic presidents than the United States. Why is modernity a boon for Catholicism in South Korea but not in Ireland? In part it has to do with the strong role the church played in the democratization of South Korea and the rejection of decades of authoritarian government. In part it is because the church in South Korea had no baggage from the ancien régime; to reject tradition and to embrace Catholicism were not necessarily two different movements. Catholicism in South Korea, in other words, is associated with change, the opening up of a pluralistic society and the rejection of hegemony; the opposite is the case in Ireland.

In Ireland, the church and the ancien régime were held together by a number of factors, some of them economic. As Dermot Keogh has written, "Ireland's arrested economic development had a number of interesting consequences, not least being the artificial conservation of a traditional society where religious observance was anomalous compared with patterns of religious observance in Western Europe."[6] Economic factors should not be overplayed—and it is not as clear as Keogh makes it sound like the vectors of causation run from economic to religious instead of the other way around—but it can be said that Irish society was marked by a paucity of choices. To be Irish was to be Catholic, and to be Catholic meant conformity to a rather inflexible code of behavior. There was much of great beauty and belonging in traditional Irish Catholicism; the caricatures do not tell the whole story by any means. Nevertheless, the institutional church exercised hegemonic influence in Irish society, and the practice of the faith in the first half of the twentieth century is often described as being marked by guilt, boundaries, negativity, conformism, fear, and lack of freedom. Holy days were a matter of obligation, not joy.[7] Vincent Twomey writes that "the main characteristic of Irish Catholicism at the beginning of the twentieth century was angelism, namely a disdain for this world in favour of the next." As a result, "Catholics in Ireland could not feel at home in the here and now; neither could they celebrate life in the present."[8]

The rapid decline of the hegemony of Catholicism in Ireland that began to gain momentum in the 1970s came on the heels of changes begun in the 1960s: the opening of the economy to external investment, the introduction of television in 1962, educational reform, the Second Vatican Council, and a number of other convulsions in Irish society.[9] In many ways, the 1960s were the pivotal decade, as they were in so many other Western countries. The legendary Archbishop McQuaid returned from Vatican II in 1965 and reassured Irish society, "No change will worry the tranquility of your Christian lives."[10] But change was already happening. Subsequently, the Celtic Tiger economy and subsequent crash and the revelations of sexual abuse and cover-up in the church have in different ways contributed to the end of Catholic domination in Ireland. In politics, academics, and the media, there are alternative and often antagonistic narratives to the Catholic one on offer, and there are now many ways to be Irish that do not include being Catholic.[11] Identity is now a consumer choice; optionality and plurality would appear to be the new normal.

It is not so clear, however, that the current situation should be described as pluralistic. Twomey notes the "institutionalised conformity" in secularized Irish politics with regard to social issues.[12] He also comments that the Irish media are uniformly hostile to the church: "To be interviewed by an Irish journalist is more an interrogation by the thought-police, and any slip-up can be fatal."[13] Many Irish elites practice what Charles Taylor calls "closed secularism," the idea that the church needs to be excluded from public relevance rather than allowed to be one voice among many in a newly pluralized society. The irony is that such closed secularism may in fact be the legacy of Catholic Ireland; Ireland may have traded one form of conformity for another. In an interview, Taylor suggests that closed secularism may be more prevalent in Europe than in the United States precisely because of the heritage of confessional states in Europe. Totally Calvinist and totally Catholic societies placed great emphasis on conforming to belong. Closed secularism has similarly totalizing ambitions. As Taylor comments, "Hard secularists like the Jacobins couldn't envision any other structure. So they had to swap one total society for another. . . . How can we run a society if we don't agree on these fundamental things? . . . In some sense, closed secularism is still in the mindset of confessional states, only we change the confession."[14]

OPTIONALITY AND HEGEMONY

A description of the new confession of secularism could take many forms. I would like to concentrate on McGurk's suggestion that consumerism has replaced Christianity. It is too simple to suggest that people have swapped worship of God for worship of iPhones. It is more the case, as Taylor puts it, that one social imaginary has been replaced with another, which changes not simply *what* people believe but *how* they believe. Taylor contends that the standard "subtraction" narrative of secularization is false. This is the common notion that the secular is a natural substrate that remains when the fantastical ideas of the supernatural are finally shed. This narrative is appealing because it is self-congratulatory ("We have finally grown up and rid ourselves of childish superstitions"), it is dramatic, with heroes and villains (put Archbishop McQuaid in the latter camp), and it is liberatory ("We are freed up once the repression by the church is lifted"). But Taylor makes a detailed and compelling historical case that the secular is not a natural remainder once religion is subtracted; it is rather a new social imaginary that is a product of changes within Christianity itself.[15] The disenchantment of the exterior material world is, Taylor argues, a product of a new late medieval and early modern emphasis on reform of the interior Christian self. Meaning becomes located in the self, not the external world, and selves thereby become "buffered" from the spiritual world and disembedded from their social context. In time, the sacramental view of the world fades, and society becomes a collection of individuals exercising their individual power of choice.

We have been taught to associate choice with liberation, but if optionality is the new hegemony, we are faced with a paradox. According to Taylor, "The process of disenchantment is irreversible."[16] By this, he does not mean that we can no longer believe in God but that to believe or not to believe in God has become a choice that we must make. God is one option among others. According to Taylor, "The main feature of this new context is that it puts an end to the naïve acknowledgement of the transcendent, or of goals or claims which go beyond human flourishing. But this is quite unlike religious turnovers in the past, where one naïve horizon ends up replacing another, or the two fuse syncretistically.... Naïveté is now unavailable to anyone, believer or unbeliever alike."[17] Taylor presents the loss of naïveté as an irreversible shift in time: "The frameworks of yesterday and today are related as 'naïve' and 'reflective', because the latter has opened a question which had been foreclosed in the former by the unacknowledged shape of the background."[18] On the other hand, however, Taylor recognizes other kinds of naïveté, such as the notion that all meaning takes place in the mind and is not located outside the mind in the world of spirits, demons, and moral forces. Taylor writes, "What I am trying to describe here is not a theory. Rather my target is our contemporary lived understanding; that is, the way we naïvely take things to be. We might say: the construal we just live in, without ever being aware of it as a construal, or—for most of us—without ever even formulating it."[19] Naïveté, it seems, is not only available, but inescapable for us in the modern West, despite what Taylor has written only a few pages before. He goes on to explain:

> I am interested in the naïve understanding, because my claim will be that a fundamental shift has occurred in naïve understanding in the move to disenchantment. This is unlike what I said above on the issue of the existence of God and other spiritual creatures. There we have moved from a naïve acceptance of their reality, to a sense that either to affirm or deny them is to enter a disputed terrain; there are no more naïve theists, just as there are no naïve atheists. But underlying this change is the one I am now talking about in our sense of our world, from one in which these spirits were just unproblematically there, impinging on us, to one in which they are no longer so, and indeed, in which many of the ways they were there have become inconceivable. Their not so impinging is what we experience naïvely.[20]

What Taylor does not directly acknowledge but seems like a logical consequence of his description of the secularized world is that optionality is also something we experience naively, if we have no choice but to choose. If the move to optionality is irreversible, then optionality is the new naïveté; optionality is not optional. What this means is that the grown-up subject of the standard subtraction narrative of secularization—the one who is now fully self-aware and liberated from naïveté—is a fiction. Hent de Vries asks:

> Does the tacit character of background framing—the "taken-for-granted" of which Taylor speaks—differ significantly in the two (naïve and reflective) ages? Or does any belief, any engagement, imply that I immediately blot out the very background, precisely

since the moment we hold any view or adopt any course of action, however habitualized, we must take for granted at least some things—indeed, a vast majority of things—even if we can never attain the level of explicitness that a meaningful use of "reflection" or "optionality" would require?[21]

As de Vries comments, if optionality cannot be rejected, then

> paradoxically, secular optionality would be somewhat of a naïveté—the very myth and opinion, superstition and dogma, credulity and fideism—of our time. In any case, its regime of possibilities would not be something about which we can reflectively—or, more precisely, discursively—think and live or act upon as such or throughout. That is to say, if there were ever such a thing as optionality, then it could never leave behind a certain level of implicitness, an unthought and lack of choice, of sorts. Its eventual expression could never satisfy our need for discursive articulation and conceptual explicitness.[22]

One possible implication of this analysis is that optionality is something with *power over us*. If we cannot opt out of optionality and indeed cannot even fully come to know and express it, then it escapes our power to control it. The inability to subject something to our control and knowledge is not necessarily a debilitating condition. There are all kinds of things—indeed a "vast majority of things," as de Vries points out—that we must take for granted in order to operate in the world. The problem is that the ideology of optionality and choice implies a level of explicitness that can never be attained. The power is in the ideology, not the "fact," of optionality. The power that optionality exerts is in part due to our inability to see and name that power. It is a power that always operates behind our backs. Because it is the new naïveté, it is nearly impossible to name that power as anything other than freedom.

CONSUMERISM AND CONFORMITY

The crucial decade—in Taylor's as in so many other narratives about the contemporary West—is the 1960s. The sixties ushered in what Taylor calls the "Age of Authenticity," a new era of "expressive" individualism. The central idea is that each person has their own way of realizing their own humanity. This type of individualism is not entirely new; it had antecedents in the nineteenth-century Romantic period and in the Bloomsbury group in the early twentieth century. What was new in the 1960s is that expressive individualism became a mass phenomenon.[23] Beyond the events of the 1960s themselves, an entire narrative of mass cultural shift in the West has crystallized around that decade, with certain well-worn cultural tropes—Woodstock, hippies in San Francisco, students at the barricades in Paris—being used to signify upheaval in the West.

In both the popular imagination and in more scholarly narratives, the 1960s are usually juxtaposed to the 1950s in stark terms. Expressive individualism is nothing without its putative opposite, which is conformity and consensus.[24] The 1950s are characterized by stifling uniformity, Levittown and Wonder Bread.[25] The basic contrast of 1950s conformity and 1960s rebellion dominates narratives both negative and positive. For some on the right, the 1960s represent a radical break with the virtuous foundations of Western civilization. In the view of Newt Gingrich, for example, the 1960s represent everything the Republican Party stands against: the erosion of consensus, community, patriotism, traditional morality, and the virtues of hard work that led to postwar prosperity.[26] The opposite narrative lionizes the sixties for the way in which the dull conformity of the previous era was broken, and people finally were able to express their individuality. The sixties counterculture is so popular that it is used to sell products, like Coca-Cola's Fruitopia line of drinks. As in the 1998 movie *Pleasantville*, set in an idyllic 1950s Iowa town, the 1950s are depicted as happening in black-and-white. In the film, two teenagers from the present become trapped in the town. As they exhibit anomalous and rebellious behavior, such as having sex with teens from the high school, the newly independent people begin to turn from black-and-white to color. The repressed leaders of the town soon organize a meeting, under a vaguely fascist-looking banner, to put a stop to all the color. Soon people are roaming the street, harassing people of color and burning books. The newcomers in *Pleasantville* represent the Age of Authenticity. As one commentator wrote, "In *Pleasantville*, color represents the transformation from repression to enlightenment. People—and their surroundings—change from black-and-white to color when they connect with the essence of who they really are." Both the negative and positive ways of narrating this massive cultural shift agree on the nature of the shift: it represents rebellion and individualism against conformity and consensus. The dissolution of consensus can be lamented or celebrated, but it is assumed to be a fact.

Commentators have placed consumerism on both sides of the conformity/individuality divide. The rise of McDonald's symbolizes postwar homogenization and the mass production of consumer goods. For Marxist critics like Jean Baudrillard, the periodic crises of capitalist overproduction must be met by creating consumer desire so that the excess goods can be sold: "The industrial system, having socialised the masses as a labour force, was forced to go further, in order to finish the job, and socialise them (which is to say, control them) as a consumption force."[27] Marketing is the primary means of this type of social control, and mass production must be complemented by mass consumption. "Mass" here indicates not simply large in quantity, but an obsession with conformity. Just as Fordist and Taylorist regimes of production tried to eliminate all individual initiative and self-determination from the production process, so marketing was aimed at the creation of predictable and standardized consumer behavior. As Baudrillard put it, "The system can only produce and reproduce individuals as elements of the system. It cannot tolerate exceptions."[28]

On the other hand, however, consumerism has been narrated as one of the primary drivers of nonconformity in postwar Western society. As Charles Taylor writes near the beginning of his chapter on the Age of Authenticity, "One of the most obvious manifestations of the individuation in question here has been the consumer revolution."[29] The multiplication of goods and services on offer in the postwar period led to a concentration on filling private space, a "newly individuated space" in which the consumer was encouraged to express his or her individual taste. Close-knit communities, extended families, and networks of mutual help began to decay, a process that Taylor labels "disembedding." Consumerism, Taylor writes, "seems to have had a tremendous appeal for populations which had been living since time out of mind under the grip of what appeared unchanging necessity, where the most optimistic horizon was maintaining a level of modest sufficiency and avoiding disaster."[30] Taylor cites Yves Lambert's study of a Breton parish in which a formerly dense communal-ritual life has given way to the pursuit of individual prosperity: "Why would I go to mass, they say to themselves, when my next-door neighbour is doing as well as me, perhaps even better, and he doesn't go."[31] In traditional society, economic, social, and spiritual lives were so closely intertwined that a change in economy must mean a change in the practice of the faith. An individual path to prosperity means that the communal rituals of Breton Catholicism were no longer necessary. A Breton interviewed by Lambert said, "We no longer have time to care about that [religion]. One seeks money, comfort, and all that; everyone is now into that, and the rest, bah!"[32] It is not very hard to imagine similar sentiments coming from an Irishman at the height of the Celtic Tiger.

The breakdown of traditional society in the West that is associated with the 1960s accompanied a strong shift in consumerism toward nonconformity. The 1950s were often pilloried as a time of stifling uniformity and bland conformism. Even such a mainstream magazine as *Life* in the United States ran a series of articles in 1967 titled "Modern Society's Growing Challenge: The Struggle to Be an Individual."[33] Thomas Frank has shown in great detail how advertising changed in the 1960s as part of a rebellion in marketing culture against the over-organization, hierarchy, and dullness of the corporation, stereotyped as ranks of boring white men in gray flannel suits.[34] In the culture wars begun in the 1960s, business was seen as "square." The movement from "square" to "hip" was a mass movement embraced enthusiastically not only by hippies but also by middle-class suburbanites, and their primary access to hip culture was through acts of consumption.

By the 1950s, the self-image of advertising as science had been well established among the leading advertising firms and theorists. Advertising was produced according to proven and fixed principles and based on scientific research on the behavior and attitudes of the public. Practitioners and critics of advertising alike saw it as the rational manipulation of passive consumers. Thus Edward Bernays's "scientific" advertising textbook, *The Engineering of Consent* (1955), was mirrored by Vance Packard's *The Hidden Persuaders* (1957), an exposé of advertisers' attempts to manipulate gullible consumers.[35] Baudrillard belongs to the same tradition of critique. Some subversive voices in the business world began to critique this icy conformism in the 1950s, however, and in the 1960s there emerged an entirely new genre of advertising as a critique of mass culture. Led by pioneering figures like Bill Bernbach, advertising now began to be self-consciously hip, to appeal to the desires of individuals to be unfettered from societal control, to express themselves through their purchases. Advertising began to glorify youth culture and disdain tradition, to mock conformity and appeal to individuality. Taylor quotes a beer commercial of the early 1970s: "Be yourselves in the world of today."[36] Products were advertised not as helping people fit in but as helping them stand out from the crowd. "Camel Filters: They're not for everybody" seems like an odd way to advertise if one's goal is to sell as many Camel cigarettes as possible. But advertising came to harness the public's mistrust of advertising and consumerism more generally. Advertisers developed a whole genre of anti-advertising advertising that mocked traditional advertising.[37] The message was usually some version of the following: you know better than to fall for the fake promises of advertising; you are not a sheep like the others; you make your own choices, and we applaud you for being one of the few who are clever enough to choose our product. "Image is nothing. Obey your thirst," as Sprite ads in the 1990s admonished us.

As this last example indicates, this genre of anti-advertising advertising did not disappear with the 1960s but has become a staple of consumer culture. Consumerism is propelled in part by the rejection of consumerism and the critique of mass society. This is just one example of the kind of rebel consumerism that has come to predominate. Consumerism is all about encouraging discontent and celebrating difference and individuality. Counterculture is now a permanent feature of consumerism. Burger King says, "Sometimes you gotta break the rules." Outback Steakhouse goes further and claims to do away with rules altogether: "No rules. Just right." This Dodge truck is a bad boy that doesn't share with its class. And so on and on. This nonconformity is not an accidental feature of contemporary advertising; it is embedded in the structures of consumer capitalism itself. Baudrillard had the critique of mass consumerism backward. The way to grease the wheels of production is not to get everyone to buy the same things. The way to keep production moving is to keep consumer desire constantly on the move. Consumerism must foster discontent with products and the constant desire to seek something new. We must be constantly ready to cast off our possessions in the pursuit of what is different, because different is always better. Change, restlessness, difference, rebellion—all work to create the demand on which production depends.

The rebel counterculture begins as discontent with consumerism itself. Disgust with mass society propels the search for style. One seeks to be a rebel, to stand out from the crowd. Goods are valued because they create a sense of distinction and superiority over the mass of conformists. One adopts bell-bottoms and tie-dye in the 1960s or grunge style in the 1990s or tattoos in the 2010s because they make a statement and set the wearer off against the crowd.[38] The problem in a society that values individuality above all is that people will immediately flock toward that which sets them apart from the crowd, and the countercultural fashions will become mainstream. The problem is that not everyone can be a rebel. As Joseph Heath and Andrew Potter point out, "If everyone joins the counterculture, then the counterculture simply becomes the culture."[39] When this happens, it then becomes necessary to find a new counterculture, but the counterculture depends on having a culture to counter, just as being a rebel depends on having rules to break. Nonconformity always depends on conformity; optionality only exists in the presence of some things that are not optional.

CONSUMERISM AND POWER

The problem of nonconformist consumerism is often dealt with according to a narrative of co-optation: the 1960s were a potential moment of true liberation from the oppression of mass society, but business saw an opportunity and co-opted the counterculture for profit. Soon hippies would want to "Buy the world a Coke," and Led Zeppelin's song "Rock and Roll" would be used to sell Cadillacs.[40] But Frank argues that "co-optation" is the wrong narrative to tell if it implies that there was a "real" counterculture that was later used by capitalism for "fake" ends. The lines between real and fake culture are very hard to draw, and Frank points out that the rise of the sixties counterculture was a mass movement from the start, triggered just as much by shifts in mass culture—like the advent of the Beatles—as by grassroots developments.[41] The liberated Pepsi Generation, rebels who embraced the new against the stuffy mores of the past, was the creation of an ad campaign launched in 1961, well before the ferment of the decade became a cultural trope. One of the admen who created the campaign later expressed feelings of guilt for having fomented some of the rebelliousness and divisiveness of the 1960s.[42] While his guilt was probably exaggerated, the larger point is that corporations were not simply mimicking what youth culture was doing, but they helped to shape it, often in response to some of the new rebel theories of management and marketing that began to circulate in corporate culture in the late 1950s.

The point is not that consumerism is a grand conspiracy of mind control directed by a few devious advertising executives but that since the 1980s there has been a reaction in academic circles against some of the traditional critiques of consumerism by such figures as Baudrillard, Thorstein Veblen, Kenneth Galbraith, Theodor Adorno, and Max Horkheimer. These thinkers have been criticized for seeing consumer society as homogeneous, for being elitist, and for seeing consumers as mindless dupes. A whole new wave of scholarly studies at the micro level has emphasized the active agency of consumers, the way that they consciously use consumption to shape their own identities and meanings. The consumer was recast as an adventurous individual trying on and casting off identities without undue regard for status. The more recent view is an important correction to some of the more heavy-handed older views; consumers are not simply idiots or dupes. As Juliet Schor has argued, however, the more recent views of the agency of consumers have a tendency to concentrate on the micro level at the expense of the macro level, or simply to conflate the two. As a result, these analyses tend to be depoliticized and unable to account for the power that producers wield in the marketplace. At the micro level, consumers may be conscious and active, but at the macro level they reproduce predictable class-based outcomes, outcomes that are in part anticipated and engineered by producers. As Schor writes:

> If we accept the view that individual agency is now central to the operation of consumer society (in contrast to an earlier era in which there was more overt social conformity), it is the companies who figure out how to successfully sell agency to consumers that thrive. In this formulation, subjectivity does not exist prior to the market (à la neoclassical economics) but is a product of it. This does not make subjectivity "false" as in earlier critiques, but it does imply that subjectivity is constrained and market driven. After all, only certain forms of subjectivity are profitable. So while consumers have gained one kind of power (market innovations begin with them), they have lost the power to reject consumption as a way of life. They are trained from the earliest ages to be consumers, and it becomes

nearly impossible to construct identity outside the consumer marketplace.[43]

If Schor is right here, then we are returned to the hegemony of optionality. Consumers have many options, but they cannot reject optionality and the way that optionality forms their identities as consumers. Optionality indeed cannot be rejected because we are not even fully conscious of it; it remains as an unthought because it constructs—rather than is constructed by—consumer subjectivity.

The point again is not that consumers are brainwashed dupes but that choice and nonconformity are simply components of the dominant economic system, which Joseph Schumpeter famously defined as "creative destruction." We are free, but we exercise our freedom in a context dominated by corporate power, which has grown through increasing consolidation, the dismantling of state regulations, the saturation of the symbol system of society with marketing (cell phones are a key facilitator of this saturation), and the signing of international treaties that favor corporate freedom over democratic controls, labor rights, and environmental protection. As Schor comments, "It is striking that this growing power has been accompanied by the dominance of an ideology that posits the reverse—that the consumer is king and the corporation is at his or her mercy."[44]

Both Frank and Taylor comment on the apparent contradiction between the self-expression encouraged in the consumer sphere and the discipline and sublimation of desire that continues to be required in the workplace.[45] If the above analysis is correct, however, there really is no contradiction. Being a rebel consumer is perfectly compatible with being a cog in a cubicle at work, because, from a macro point of view, both serve to keep the wheels of production spinning. Indeed, the disembedding of people from communities—town, family, church, and so on—that accompanies the rise of rebel consumerism is essential to contemporary capitalism, which demands mobility and a "flexible" workforce. Premodern communities are marked by mutual responsibilities and communal rituals; people are in each other's business, for better and for worse. Modernity shakes individuals loose from such forms of communal life, motivated— to an extent that goes largely unrecognized by Taylor—by the enclosure of common lands, the rise of wage labor, urbanization, and other creatively destructive effects of capitalism. The process has only been accelerated by the various forms of new economy, in which capital is liquid and borderless, and people can make purchases online without ever encountering another human being. The disembedding of individuals from communities liberates people to make their own choices about whom to associate with, what to eat and wear, how to express one's sexuality, what to celebrate and when, and whether or not to sleep late on Sunday morning. This is precisely what Taylor means by optionality. The move from rural communities in which social networks are strong to urban environments where anonymity is easy and viability depends entirely on one's income lends itself to the commodification of relationships. People establish relationships of meaning with products and brands—and mediate their relationships with other people through their relationships with consumer items—precisely to the extent that face-to-face relationships with other people are attenuated.

This move from community to immunity, to use the economist Luigino Bruni's terms, is typically narrated as liberation. Adam Smith thought that the impersonal market would rescue people from having to depend on the benevolence of others; he saw immunity as a great leap forward over the hierarchical and static relationships of the medieval period.[46] The market promises freedom from the risk of relationships, from the wounds that the other can inflict, but Smith did not envision a society without love. Indeed, freedom from obligation means that *philia* is now voluntary, and therefore a higher form of love.[47] Nevertheless, as Bruni points out, love in a modern economy is considered a scarce resource; the underlying principle is "let love not do what the market can do." "This allows love to be 'saved up' and then be used in private where it has no good substitutes."[48] In the market, I approach every transaction not as a person vulnerable to the risk of relationship but as a sovereign rational chooser exercising its freedom.

There is no question that there are advantages for many people in this process of disembedding. In many traditional societies, the gender, family, social, and economic roles over which people have little choice are experienced as confining. There is a lack of reciprocity in many kinds of hierarchy that is oppressive. All of this is easily identified. What is harder to identify are the types of discipline that operate in an economy that is so consistently touted as free. This is the unthought of optionality that struggles to be expressed. If optionality is not optional, then there is at least the possibility that not everyone will experience optionality as liberating.

As Taylor writes, "While remaining aware of the attractions of the new culture, we must never underestimate the ways in which one can also be forced into it: the village community disintegrates, the local factory closes, jobs disappear in 'downsizing,' the immense weight of social approval and opprobrium begins to tell on the side of the new individualism."[49]

There are many manifestations of coercion in a capitalist society. The very depersonalization of the market leaves people feeling that it is a force beyond anyone's control, to which we must simply bow as to our fate. Though the market mechanism is based on the destruction of hierarchy, the corporation remains the most rigidly hierarchical modern institution. As Bruni points out, the hierarchy of the corporation is a means to the end of maximizing profits, which is regarded as the only end of the corporation. The depersonalized maximization of profits is an effect of the same immunizing effect that destroys market hierarchies: "The capitalist enterprise and the market are two mechanisms that aim at avoiding being wounded by the other."[50] Managers of corporations furthermore regard themselves as not only subject to their superiors, but subject to impersonal "market forces" that insist that the maximization of profit be prioritized regardless of the price that workers and the environment might have to pay. When managers move jobs to where cheaper labor can be exploited, they do so not freely but under the dictatorial demands of those impersonal "market forces." For this reason, Adam Smith regarded the free market, as Robert Heilbroner put it, as "the strictest taskmaster of all. One may appeal the ruling of a planning board or win the dispensation of a minister; but there is no appeal, no dispensation, from the anonymous pressures of the market mechanism."[51]

In the sphere of consumption, however, social control in late capitalist societies now largely is experienced not as coercion but as what Zygmunt Bauman calls "seduction." Seduction in this sense is not being offered concrete rewards or urged to adopt a new ideology. More specifically, late capitalism offers an ever expanding horizon of choice. Needs are not necessarily met—in some cases and for some classes of people, communist societies are better at meeting basic material needs—but late capitalism is better at *multiplying needs*. There is a much broader range of *potential* fulfillments, and being able to choose which ones among them to pursue gives the consumer self a sense of agency and freedom that more embedded selves do not have.[52] As Taylor comments, "All this conformity and alienation may nevertheless feel like choice and self-determination; not only because consumer spaces with their multiplying options celebrate choice, but also because in embracing some style within them, I may feel myself to be breaking out of some more confining space of family or tradition."[53] In the case of Ireland, it is the feeling of confinement produced by the traditional church that makes the narrative of liberation by optionality so much more plausible.

CONSUMERISM AND MAGIC

At this point, it is worth reiterating that there is no going back to the Catholic consensus that once dominated Ireland, a consensus that produced both holiness and distortions of church and society. I have long argued against cozy relationships between church and state, and I am convinced that the gospel is often twisted when the church becomes part of the power structure. Freedom to practice one's faith or none at all is a good. As Taylor sensibly comments on the broader changes across the West since the 1950s, there are both gains and losses, and they need to be carefully considered. Taylor thinks that the changes are, on balance, positive, but there is no point to embracing slogans like "freedom," "choice," and "individuality" as if they were unambiguous goods. Any society needs consensus on some issues and choices on others, conformity in some areas and not in others, certain kinds of rights and other kinds of duties, and so on. The question is always, which ones, and at what cost? Taylor wisely wants to avoid both a resentful nostalgia that sees even the positive aspirations of modernity to self-expression as nothing but illusion and an uncritical embrace of the Age of Authenticity as if it were cost-free and incapable of being trivialized. Taylor emphasizes that there are some options that are no longer available to us, but at the same time we do have options in the new context, some better than others. "Root and branch attacks on authenticity help to make our lives worse, while being powerless to put the clock back to an earlier time."[54]

I am in complete sympathy with Taylor's balanced approach. For the church to declare itself opposed to the prevailing culture is a dead end, one that ironically mirrors the cul-de-sac that the attempt to be countercultural—analyzed above—traps us in. I am not convinced, however, that

Taylor has fully appreciated the paradox of optionality. On the one hand, he wants to convince us that we have plenty of good options in the new context, and we do not have simply to decide for or against the new Age of Authenticity. On the other hand, however, he has declared that optionality is simply the way it is now, and there is no questioning the new dispensation. I am afraid that this leaves us in a situation of exercising options within the limits set by a mandatory acceptance of a larger economic-political-cultural system that becomes unquestionable. Like Schor, I worry that we will believe there is no resistance possible to the dominant system of corporate capitalism. At the macro level, we simply need to accept that "creative destruction" is our fate and that capitalism in its current form is like global warming in the fantasies of climate change deniers, that is, something over which humans have no control. We simply need to accept its inevitability.

I don't think this is where Taylor wants to end up, but I think he is in danger of ending up here because he presents the Age of Authenticity as the product of human aspirations to self-expression and vastly understates the role of capitalism in its production. Indeed, capitalism plays a very small role in Taylor's narrative. He does, however, make a very interesting comment in his discussion of the rise of postwar consumerism and the decay of traditional Breton society: "It is almost as though the 'conversion' was a response to a stronger form of magic, as earlier conversions had been."[55] The "almost" in this sentence protects Taylor's contention that modernity has been disenchanted and there is no turning back. But Taylor seems to intuit that consumerism has a power over us that, if not simply compulsory, is difficult to resist. His language of consumerism as a stronger form of magic in fact calls into question his sharp dichotomies between enchantment and disenchantment, religious and secular, and it also questions the irreversibility of the shift from premodern to modern, or traditional to disembedded. Consumerism is an altered form of the sacramentality that modernity is supposed to have vanquished.

The idea of consumerism as a kind of magic or religion is of course not a new idea. Karl Marx famously critiqued "commodity fetishism," seeking to explain the attraction of products by analogy with "the misty realm of religion."[56] Pope Francis has denounced the false religion of the market.[57] Empirical studies have shown that consumption in Western societies has become a substitute for traditional religion and a way in which people express sacred aspirations.[58] Jackson Lears's cultural history of advertising has emphasized the survival and flourishing in modernity of what he calls the "animistic" worldview, that is, the view that material objects are used by people to express and control fantasies, fables, and broader visions of the good life.[59] These analyses are quite different from one another, but all are free of Taylor's "almost" and thus leave open some options that Taylor seems to foreclose. If the church can recognize in consumerism a different kind of religion, then a simultaneously more incisive and more sympathetic critique and pastoral plan can emerge.

A few ideas for such a pastoral plan are as follows. First, seeing consumerism as a "stronger form of magic" would help to get our description of what is going on right. Rather than acquiesce to the common narrative of church mystification and oppression versus consumer autonomy and freedom, we are able to see that consumerism produces its own kinds of mystification. Consumer culture, while not without its advantages, produces its own forms of conformity, hierarchy, and power. The hegemony of optionality could be brought to some kind of conceptual explicitness, and the playing field between consumerism and Christianity could be leveled.

Second, if consumerism as the retail expression of global capitalism is powerful but not simply inevitable, then the church can help promote alternatives. There can be a political response that insists on limits to corporate power and refuses to accept the conflation of citizens and consumers, one that pushes back against the increasing merging of state and corporate power, what Pope Benedict XVI called the "state-and-market binary." The church can promote what Benedict called "dispersed political authority" and grassroots experiments in new forms of economy that put love at the center.[60] The church's response to consumerism can never rest with critique but must always advance alternative kinds of community that make living the gospel easier.

Third, if the "conversion" to consumerism was, as Taylor hints, "a response to a stronger form of magic, as earlier conversions had been," then it is at least possible that the earlier type of conversion is not yet a dead option. In order to make such conversions possible today, however, the church will have to wield not just a stronger form of magic, but a better one. The church will have to overcome its tendency to what Twomey calls angelism by making people feel at home in this beautiful world that God has created. The sacramental heart of the Catholic faith will have to be reinvigorated, for it is the sacraments that not only display "magic" as something from out of this world but also show that God is pleased to be found in the material stuff of this world, in the fruit of the vine and the work of human hands, in bread, wine, water, and all the everyday things that our bodies encounter. The church will have to leave behind the world of imposed consensus and learn to value what is good about the aspiration to freedom and authenticity. The church will have to appreciate the long-ing for transcendence in material things that consumerism evinces while simultaneously inviting such desire to find its resting place in God, who generously offers grace in sacramental form, that is, in the material world. The only true response the church can offer to consumerism is a better freedom and a better delight in God's good creation.

NOTES

1. Tom McGurk, "Land of Brands and Consumers," *Sunday Business Post*, September 2, 2000. The online version of the article I accessed lists the author as "Anonymous," but Vincent Twomey identifies the author as McGurk: D. Vincent Twomey, SVD, *The End of Irish Catholicism?* (Dublin: Veritas, 2003), 194n27.

2. National Conference of Priests of Ireland, "Statement," *The Furrow* 29, no. 6 (June 1978): 382–83.

3. Charles Taylor, *A Secular Age* (Cambridge, MA: Harvard University Press, 2007), 3.

4. Michele Dillon, "Secularization, Generational Change, and Ireland's Post-Secular Opportunity," in *The Catholic Church in Ireland Today*, ed. David Carroll Cochran and John C. Waldmeir (Lanham, MD: Lexington Books, 2015), 49.

5. See, e.g., Leslie Woodcock Tentler, ed., *The Church Confronts Modernity: Catholicism since 1950 in the United States, Ireland, and Quebec* (Washington, DC: Catholic University of America Press, 2007).

6. Dermot Keogh, "Ireland since the 1950s," in Tentler, *The Church Confronts Modernity*, 94–95.

7. For examples of this type of characterization of traditional Irish Catholi-cism, see Eamon Maher, "Faith of Our Fathers: A Lost Legacy?," in Cochran and Waldmeir, *The Catholic Church in Ireland Today*, 9–10; Keogh, "Ireland since the 1950s," 99–109; Twomey, *End of Irish Catholicism?*, 32–34.

8. Twomey, *End of Irish Catholicism?*, 75.

9. Keogh, "Ireland since the 1950s," 110–11.

10. John Charles McQuaid, quoted in Keogh, "Ireland since the 1950s," 110–11.

11. See Lawrence Taylor, "Crisis of Faith or Collapse of Empire?," in Tentler, *The Church Confronts Modernity*, 172–73.

12. Twomey, *End of Irish Catholicism?*, 71.

13. Ibid., 67.

14. Charles Taylor, interview with James K.A. Smith, "Imagining an 'Open' Secularism," *Comment* (Fall 2014), www.cardus.ca/comment/article/4645/imagining-an-open-secularism/.

15. Taylor, *Secular Age*, 22: "I will be making a continuing polemic against what I call 'subtraction stories.' Concisely put, I mean by this, stories of modernity in general, and secularity in particular, which explain them by human beings having lost, or sloughed off, or liberated themselves from certain earlier, confining horizons, or illusions, or limitations of knowledge. What emerges from this process—modernity or secularity—is to be understood in terms of underlying features of human nature which were there all along, but had been impeded by what is now set aside. Against this kind of story, I will steadily be arguing that Western modernity, including its secularity, is the fruit of new inventions, newly constructed self-understandings and related practices, and cannot be explained in terms of perennial features of human life."

16. Charles Taylor, "Disenchantment-Reenchantment," in *The Joy of Secularism: 11 Essays for How We Live Now*, ed. George Levine (Princeton, NJ: Princeton University Press, 2011), 57.

17. Taylor, *Secular Age*, 21. I also discuss Taylor on optionality in my chapter "Sacrament, Enchantment, and Idolatry: Looking for Grace in the Secular," in the forthcoming volume *Grace, Governance, and Globalization*.

18. Taylor, *Secular Age*, 13.

19. Ibid., 30.

20. Ibid.

21. Hent de Vries, "The Deep Conditions of Secularity," *Modern Theology* 26, no. 3 (July 2010): 393.

22. Ibid., 392.

23. Taylor, *Secular Age*, 473–76.

24. Ibid., 476.

25. Levittown is the name given to a post–World War II uniform housing scheme, and Wonder Bread refers to the bread sold nationwide in North America, first sold in 1921 and then sold pre-sliced beginning in 1930.

26. See Thomas Frank, *The Conquest of Cool: Business Culture, Counterculture, and the Rise of Hip Consumerism* (Chicago: University of Chicago Press, 1997), 2–3. Although Frank's book and much of my analysis that follows is based on examples from the American context, the overall movement from the 1960s to the present is generalizable across what we call "the Western world," although the changes in places like Ireland may have come slightly later.

27. Jean Baudrillard, *La société de consommation* (Paris: Éditions Denoël, 1970), 115; translation found in Joseph Heath and Andrew Potter, *The Rebel Sell* (Chichester: Capstone Publishing, 2006), 109–10.

28. Jean Baudrillard, "The Ideological Genesis of Needs," trans. Charles Levin, in *The Consumer Society Reader*, ed. Juliet B. Schor and Douglas B. Holt (New York: New Press, 2000), 77; quoted in Heath and Potter, *Rebel Sell*, 110.

29. Taylor, *Secular Age*, 474.

30. Ibid., 490.

31. This quote is cited from Lambert's study in Taylor, *Secular Age*, 490.

32. Ibid.

33. Frank, *Conquest of Cool*, 13. As Heath and Potter, *Rebel Sell*, 26–30, point out, the rage against conformity in the 1960s was fed by the well-known experiments of Stanley Milgram and Hannah Arendt's *Eichmann in Jerusalem*, which revealed a disturbing human tendency to follow orders blindly, as well as a reaction against totalitarianism fed by literary works like George Orwell's *1984* and Aldous Huxley's *Brave New World*.

34. Frank, *Conquest of Cool*, 9.

35. Ibid., 39–40.

36. Taylor, *Secular Age*, 475.

37. Frank, *Conquest of Cool*, 54–55. Frank echoes Mark Crispin Miller's critique of television: "TV preempts derision by itself evincing endless irony.... TV protects its ads from mockery by doing all the mocking, thereby posing as an ally to the incredulous spectator" (quoted in Frank, *Conquest of Cool*, 231).

38. For more on the way that novelty and disappointment with novelty operates in consumerism, see Colin Campbell, *The Romantic Ethic and the Spirit of Modern Consumerism* (Oxford: Blackwell, 1987).

39. Heath and Potter, *Rebel Sell*, 130.

40. The ads can be seen at www.youtube.com/watch?v=1VM2eLhvsSM (1971) and www.youtube.com/watch?v=bIOhgZswp8M (2002).

41. Frank, *Conquest of Cool*, 7–9.

42. Ibid., 169–74. The Pepsi campaign was launched in 1961, though the actual words "Pepsi Generation" were first applied to it in 1963.

43. Juliet B. Schor, "In Defense of Consumer Critique: Revisiting the Consumption Debates of the Twentieth Century," *Annals of the American Academy of Political and Social Science* 611 (May 2007): 25.

44. Ibid., 28.

45. Frank, *Conquest of Cool*, 232; Taylor, *Secular Age*, 493.

46. Luigino Bruni, *The Wound and the Blessing: Economic Relationships and Happiness*, trans. N. Michael Brennen (Hyde Park, NY: New City Press, 2012), 12–16.

47. Ibid., 16.

48. Ibid., 60.

49. Taylor, *Secular Age*, 492.

50. Bruni, *The Wound and the Blessing*, 30. "From a certain point of view, there exists a close continuity between a large capitalist enterprise and the market: both see themselves as surpassing the *communitas* toward *immunitas*, because both the bureaucratic hierarchy and the spontaneous coordination of prices function without

having to enter the dangerous territory of a face-to-face relationship with a personal 'Thou.'"

51. Robert Heilbroner, *The Worldly Philosophers: The Life, Times, and Ideas of the Great Economic Thinkers*, 5th ed. (New York: Simon and Schuster, 1980), 55.

52. Vincent J. Miller, *Consuming Religion: Christian Faith and Practice in a Consumer Culture* (New York: Continuum, 2004), 117.

53. Taylor, *Secular Age*, 483.

54. Ibid., 478–81.

55. Ibid., 490.

56. Karl Marx, *Capital*, trans. Ben Fowkes, 3 vols. (New York: Vintage, 1977), 1:165. "There the products of the human brain appear as autonomous figures endowed with a life of their own, which enter into relations both with each other and with the human race. So it is in the world of commodities with the products of men's hands. I call this the fetishism which attaches itself to the products of labor as soon as they are produced as commodities, and is therefore inseparable from the production of commodities."

57. Pope Francis, *Evangelii Gaudium*, §55.

58. See, e.g., Russell W. Belk, Melanie Wallendorf, and John F. Sherry Jr., "The Sacred and the Profane in Consumer Behavior: Theodicy on the Odyssey," *Journal of Consumer Research* 16 (1989): 1–38; Ron Shachar, Tülin Erdem, Keisha M. Cutright, and Gavin J. Fitzsimons, "Brands: The Opiate of the Nonreligious Masses?," *Marketing Science* 30 (2011): 92–110.

59. Jackson Lears, *Fables of Abundance: A Cultural History of Advertising in America* (New York: Basic Books, 1994).

60. Pope Benedict XVI, *Caritas in Veritate*. For my analysis of this encyclical, see chapter 6 in my book *Field Hospital: The Church's Engagement with a Wounded World* (Grand Rapids, MI: Eerdmans, 2016).

SIX

The Established Church Dilemma

MASSIMO FAGGIOLI

We are now in a new phase in the globalization of Catholicism, and it is time to reconsider the debate on the Constantinian age and the "established church" and its meaning for the church of today.[1] This is necessary in order to develop some reflections on the dilemma of the post–Vatican II church in the age of "the technocratic paradigm" that "tends to dominate economic and political life."[2] Is the church the last of those that resist this paradigm? If this is true, should the church abandon the established church system, since it is this system that grants it financial support and other special privileges? Is it not the case that it is this system that allows the church to provide our world with the last defense for the poor and the marginalized?

This chapter does *not* advocate a return of the political and religious ideology of constantinianism.[3] Rather it seeks to explore how the church's changed situation can influence our understandings of constantinianism and the established church model whereby the church enjoys a particular and privileged position in the constitutional order of the state.

VATICAN II AND THE CONSTANTINIAN AGE

The debate on the Constantinian age was a turning point in the theological and ecclesiological debate in the first half of the twentieth century. In a fine book published in 2012, the Italian German historian Gianmaria Zamagni reconstructs the genesis of the historiographical and theological argument against constantinianism.[4] It was a debate that had an influence not only on Vatican II but also on its reception. One of the master narratives of Vatican II is that it put an end to the tight relationship between Catholicism and Christendom. The influence of Marie-Dominique Chenu and of the "end of constantinianism" is undeniable in Vatican II and indeed also on the interpreters and historians of Vatican II.[5]

The position of Vatican II vis-à-vis constantinianism and the established church is more complex. Many of the bishops and theologians at Vatican II came from European countries with established Catholic churches. Among these were the bishops and theologians of the so-called progressive majority, with the notable exception of those from France, where the church was not established.[6] On the other hand, there were important groups of traditionalists, conservatives, and curial opponents to the majority from countries such as Italy, Spain, and Latin America where there was an established Catholic church.[7]

The preparatory period of Vatican II saw the schema on the church (*De ecclesia*) offer an ecclesiology that took for granted an established church as the permanent situation.[8] The first challenge to the ecclesiological and juridical model of the established church came from the growing debate on religious liberty. This debate owes much to the work of the new Secretariat for Christian Unity,[9] together with the emerging magisterial contribution on human rights of John XXIII and the developing debate on the role of church in the modern world. A key moment came in April 1963 with the publication of the encyclical *Pacem in Terris*.[10]

John XXIII's opening address, *Gaudet Mater Ecclesia* (October 11, 1962), offered a strikingly different tone from that of the official documents of the preparatory period. Pope John addressed the agenda of the council historically, speaking in a hopeful way about the future and about a "new order of human relations." Just a few lines after the famous passage against "the prophets of gloom," there is an important paragraph about the relations between the church and political power.

It suffices to leaf even cursorily through the pages of ecclesiastical history to note clearly how the Ecumenical Councils themselves, while constituting a series of true glories for the Catholic Church, were often held to the accompaniment of most serious difficulties and sufferings because of the undue interference of civil authorities. The princes of this world, indeed, sometimes in all sincerity, intended thus to protect the Church. But more frequently this occurred not without spiritual damage and danger, since their interest therein was guided by the views of a selfish and perilous policy. In this regard, we confess to you that we feel most poignant sorrow over the fact that very many bishops, so dear to us are noticeable here today by their absence, because they are imprisoned for their faithfulness to Christ, or impeded by other restraints.[11]

John XXIII set a new tone for the ecclesiology of Vatican II. His statement, "The Spouse of Christ prefers to make use of the medicine of mercy rather than that of severity," marks the church of mercy as something different from the "law and order" kind of Catholicism associated with constantinian Christendom. Moreover, he moves beyond the divisiveness between Catholics and non-Catholic Christians embedded in the established church vision. He points to solidarity between Catholics and the whole human family. Pope John's attitude toward Italian politics before becoming pope was instructive in this sense. His opening speech at Vatican II was not a total rupture from Cardinal Roncalli, as he was known before his election to the papacy.[12]

The first *Message to the World*, approved by the council fathers on October 20, 1962, contained the idea of a church engaged in the world, not protected by political power. *Gaudium et Spes* will further develop this idea.

It is far from true that because we cling to Christ we are diverted from earthly duties and toils. On the contrary, faith, hope, and the love of Christ impel us to serve our brothers, thereby, patterning ourselves after the example of the Divine Teacher, who "came not to be served but to serve" (Mt. 20:28). Hence, the church too was not born to dominate but to serve. He laid down His life for us, and we too ought to lay down our lives for our brothers (1 Jn. 3:16).

This is not an ecclesiology of a church in retreat, or in complete with-drawal: on the contrary, it denounces injustices and renews its commit-ment for a new order.

> The Supreme Pontiff also pleads for social justice. The teaching expounded in his encyclical *Mater et Magistra* clearly shows that the Church is supremely necessary for the modern world if injustices and unworthy inequalities are to be denounced, and if the true order of affairs and of values is to be restored, so that man's life can become more human according to the standards of the gospel.[13]

After the prophetic opening with *Gaudet Mater Ecclesia* and the coun-cil fathers' *Message to the World*, the church at Vatican II returned to the debates about the "constitutionalization" of its "hierarcology" (to use Yves Congar's famous definition). Ecclesiological debate at Vatican II reached its high point in October 1963. This debate was mostly concentrated on internal issues, such as the sacramentality of the episcopal order, episco-pal collegiality, and restoration of the permanent diaconate. All this was a move toward a system similar to a constitutional ecclesiology compat-ible with the established church system. During the second intersession and the third session, the commission, *de episcopis*, debated the reform of the appointment of bishops, a typical element of the established church. The Secretariat of State then stopped further discussions on the subject: a return to following the procedures for appointing bishops in the early church could have put in jeopardy the role of the Holy See in defending the freedom of the church in the communist world. A return to the older way would have envisaged a more decentralized procedure, with a more significant role for the local church and its laity. During this same period, the Holy See was dealing with communist-ruled Hungary with the aim of keeping its privileges in the appointment of bishops for a church under communism. The aim was to preserve the concordat with communist Hungary.[14]

The challenge for the established church system was coming from another front, namely, the debate on religious liberty of September 1964 and September 1965. This marked the beginning of the end of the teaching that "error has no rights."[15] During this last session, the debate on war and peace illustrated again the ramifications of the theology of the established church. This was exemplified in the debate about "just war." In the final vote, the "established" Catholic position about the moral legitimacy of nuclear weapons was represented by the bishops of the United States.[16]

Lumen Gentium did not address the issue of the established church directly. Nonetheless, the episcopalist ecclesiology of the constitution leads toward an institutional ecclesiology that reflects a juridical ecclesiology. This juridical ecclesiology comes from the experience of the established church in the modern period rather than the patristic model of the early centuries. Other documents addressed more directly the issue of the Constantinian age, especially *Gaudium et Spes*. The pastoral constitution on the church in the modern world, the last document approved by Vatican II and inspired by French theology, Chenu in particular,[17] opened with a statement about the relationship between the church and power: "The Church is not motivated by earthly ambition, but is interested in one thing only—to carry on the work of Christ under the guidance of the Holy Spirit, who came into the world to bear witness to the truth, to save and not to judge, to serve and not to be served" (*GS* 3).[18] Even clearer were the texts in chapter 4 on the life of the political community: "It is clear that the political community and public authority are based on human nature, and therefore they need to belong to an order established by God; nevertheless, the choice of the political regime and the appointment of rulers are left to the free decision of the citizens" (*GS* 74).

It follows that political authority, either within the political community as such or through organizations representing the state, must be exercised within the limits of the moral order and directed toward the common good, understood in the dynamic sense of the term, according to the juridical order legitimately established or to be established. Citizens, then, are bound in conscience to obey. Accordingly, the responsibility, the status, and the importance of the rulers of a state are clear: "When citizens are being oppressed by a public authority which oversteps its competence, they should not refuse whatever is objectively demanded of them by the common good; but it is legitimate for them to defend their own rights and those of their fellow citizens against abuses of this authority within the limits of the natural law and the law of the Gospel" (*GS* 74).

Gaudium et Spes questioned the legacy of many of the political regimes backing established Catholicism: "It is inhuman for public authority to fall back on totalitarian methods or dictatorship which violate the rights of persons or social groups" (*GS* 75). Clearer still was the following paragraph about Catholics and pluralistic society.

> It is very important, especially in a pluralist society, to have a proper understanding of the relationship between the political community and the church, and to distinguish clearly between the activities of Christians, acting individually or collectively in their own name as citizens guided by the dictates of a Christian conscience, and what they do together with their pastors in the name of the church.
>
> The Church, by reason of her role and competence, is not identified with any political community nor is it tied to any political system. It is at once the sign and the safeguard of the transcendent dimension of the human person.
>
> The political community and the church are autonomous and independent of each other in their own fields. They are both at the service of the personal and social vocation of the same individuals, though under different titles. Their service will be more efficient and beneficial to all if both institutions develop better co-operation according to the circumstances of time and place. For humanity's horizons are not confined to the temporal order; living in human history they retain the fullness of their eternal calling. The Church, for its part, being founded on the love of the Redeemer, contributes towards the spread of justice and charity among nations and in the nations themselves. By preaching the truths of the Gospel and clarifying all sectors of human activity through its teaching and the witness of its members, the church respects and encourages the political freedom and responsibility of the citizens. (*GS* 76)

Together with *Gaudium et Spes*, the declaration on religious liberty, *Dignitatis Humanae*, offered a theological perspective on the issue of church and state. *Dignitatis Humanae* espouses the idea of religious liberty as a fundamental right; this was a mortal blow to the idea of established Catholicism as it had been in some European countries (Spain and Italy especially). The first paragraph of *Dignitatis Humanae* stated: "Truth can impose itself upon the human mind by the force of its own truth, which wins over the mind with both gentleness and power. So, while the religious freedom which human beings demand in fulfilling their obligation to worship God has to do with freedom from coercion in civil society, it leaves intact the traditional Catholic teaching on the moral obligation of individuals and societies towards the true religion and the one Church of Christ" (*DH* 1).

Dignitatis Humanae paragraph 5 talked about the right of parents to free choice of school ("furthermore, the rights of parents are violated if their children are compelled to attend classes which are not in agreement with the religious beliefs of the parents or there is but a single compulsory system of education from which all religious instruction is excluded"). But it was paragraph 6 that addressed the issue of the established church most directly.

> The protection and promotion of the inviolable rights of the human person is an essential duty of every civil authority. The civil authority must therefore undertake effectively to safeguard the religious freedom of all citizens, by just legislation and other appropriate means. It must help to create conditions favorable to the fostering of religious life so that the citizens will be really in a position to exercise their religious rights and fulfill their religious duties and so that society itself may enjoy the benefits of justice and peace, which results from people's faithfulness to God and His holy will. If because of the circumstances of a particular people special civil recognition is given to one religious community in the constitutional organization of a state, the right of all citizens and religious communities to religious freedom must be recognized and respected as well.
>
> Finally, the civil authority must see to it that equality of the citizens before the law, which is itself an element of the common good of society, is never violated either openly or covertly for religious reasons and there is no discrimination between citizens. (*DH* 6)

Dignitatis Humanae did not eliminate the possibility of special civil recognition being given to one religious community in the constitutional order of society, but it clearly stated that religious freedom of other groups and the equality of citizens under the law must be respected.

Even more nuanced was the text of the decree on the bishops, *Christus Dominus*, which addressed the issue of the church's freedom to appoint bishops as well as the issue of the concordats. Paragraph 19 of *Christus Dominus* discusses the freedom of the church, as well as its collaboration with the civil authority.

> In the exercise of their apostolic function, which is directed towards the salvation of souls, bishops enjoy as of right full and perfect freedom and independence from all civil authority. It is, therefore, unlawful to obstruct them directly or indirectly in the exercise of their ecclesiastical office or to prevent them from communicating freely with the apostolic see and other ecclesiastical authorities or with their subjects.
>
> In fact, the sacred pastors in devoting themselves to the spiritual care of their flock are in fact promoting social and civil progress and prosperity. With this end in view they cooperate actively with the public authorities in a manner consonant with their office and fitting for bishops, enjoining obedience to just laws and prescribing reverence for legitimately constituted authority. (*CD* 19)

Paragraph 20 of *Christus Dominus* makes a statement about the freedom of the church and the end of an age of privileges regarding the nomination of bishops granted to some states.

> The holy ecumenical council asserts that the competent ecclesiastical authority has the proper, special, and as of right, exclusive power to appoint and install bishops. Therefore in order to safeguard the liberty of the Church and the better and the more effectively to promote the good of the faithful, it is the desire of the holy council that for the future no rights or privileges be conceded to the civil authorities in regard to the election, nomination or presentation to bishoprics. The civil authorities in question, whose good will toward the Church the sacred synod gratefully acknowledges and fully appreciates, are respectfully asked to initiate discussion with the Holy See with the object of freely waiving the aforesaid rights and privileges which they at present enjoy by agreement or custom. (*CD* 20)

Even more telling of the status quo perspective of *Christus Dominus* was the passage at paragraph 43 on military vicariates. This issue plays a key role in the church's position in the struggle between democracy and dictatorship in Latin America before and after Vatican II.[19]

> The spiritual welfare of military personnel, on account of the special nature of their life, should be the object of particular solicitude. A special military vicariate should therefore, if possible, be established in every country. The vicar and his chaplains should go about this difficult work with the utmost zeal and in harmonious cooperation with diocesan bishops.
>
> Diocesan bishops should for this purpose release to the military vicar a sufficient number of priests well equipped for this difficult work. They should also give every encouragement to undertakings intended to promote the spiritual welfare of military personnel. (*CD* 43)

The ambivalence of Vatican II on the issue of the established church was clear also in the "Message to Rulers," read along with the final messages of the council in St. Peter's Square on December 8, 1965.

> We proclaim publicly: We do honor to your authority and your sovereignty, we respect your office, we recognize your just laws, we esteem those who make them and those who apply them. But we have a sacrosanct word to speak to you and it is this: only God is great. God alone is the beginning and the end. God alone is the source of your authority and the foundation of your laws. . . . What does this Church ask of you after close to 2,000 years of experiences of all kinds in her relations with you, the powers of the earth? What does the Church ask of you today? She tells you in one of the major documents of this council. She asks of you only liberty, the liberty to believe and to preach her faith, the freedom to love her God and serve Him, the freedom to live and to bring to men her message of life. Do not fear her. She is made after the image of her Master, whose mysterious action does not interfere with your prerogatives but heals everything human of its fatal weakness, transfigures it and fills it with hope, truth and beauty. . . . We, His humble ministers, allow us to spread everywhere without hindrance the Gospel of peace on which we have meditated during this council. Of it, your

peoples will be the first beneficiaries, since the Church forms for you loyal citizens, friends of social peace and progress.[20]

Vatican II strongly reaffirmed the idea of a church of service and not of power, but not without pragmatism and caution. On the one hand, Vatican II departs from the ecclesiology of constantinianism. Freedom of conscience, and religious liberty, ecumenism, and inter-religious dialogue, these are major changes from the political-ideological arrangement of church and state in Christendom that had been given theological supports. These theological supports vanished with Vatican II. On the other hand, Vatican II did not proceed to simply disestablish unilaterally what was from the beginning a bilateral agreement between church and state. The council knew well that world politicians, ambassadors, and intelligence agencies were observing it closely.[21]

THE ESTABLISHED CHURCH AFTER VATICAN II
AND IN THE WRITINGS OF POPE FRANCIS

The changes in the Catholic Church as an institution, introduced by the ecclesiology of Vatican II, are still incomplete. Some key features of the global Catholic Church remain as legacies of European Christendom. Perhaps the most notable of these is the financial contribution the Catholic Church receives annually, from taxpayers' money, thanks to the concordats in states like Italy and Germany. The ecclesiology of Vatican II, as it was applied during the postconciliar period, resulted in some instances in maintaining an institutional status quo. However, the actual conditions of the Catholic Church today, especially in those areas where the future of world Catholicism lies—the Global South—cannot sustain such an institutional status quo. The ecclesiology of Vatican II amounts to a theological break from the system of a church supported ideologically and materially by political power. At the same time it assumes a status quo that could not, and did not intend to, change overnight: the biggest change was to come not from theology or canon law but from the world outside.

The post–Vatican II reforms did not change the overall system of relations between church and state. This holds also for those countries where the Catholic Church is an established church. There were huge cultural changes, what Stephen Schloesser has identified as the biopolitical crisis of Catholicism.[22] After Vatican II, there was a loss of political power by those Catholic and Christian Democratic parties that had re-created Europe immediately after World War II.[23] These changes, however, did not lead to a revolution in the established church system: no concordat was called into question or abrogated. There were updates to the concordats (the German concordat had been declared constitutional in 1957; in 1984 Italy and the Holy See signed a new concordat that updated the previous one), but nobody—except perhaps radical and anticlerical parties on the fringes—had an interest in spending political capital trying to completely tear down the public role of the church in Western Europe, especially before the fall of the Berlin wall. Those who believed that the age of the concordats was over after Vatican II were wrong—at least during the John Paul II era of the post–Vatican II church.[24]

After the fall of communism in 1989–91, it was not the church that occupied the space vacated by communism but the free market. During the second phase of the post–Vatican II period (which I suggest begins between 1985 and the 1990s), the social and political role of the Catholic Church in European countries changed. This was despite the attempt to slow down the impact of secularization, not only through the "new evangelization," but also through the classic diplomatic tools for the strengthening of the public role of the church.[25] The church lost its fight for a European Union, founded on the "Christian roots" of the continent, and a decade later the European Union lost its soul.[26] In the quarter of a century after the end of communism, John Paul II and then Benedict XVI had to walk a fine line. On the one hand, the Catholic Church became the most important global advocate of human rights and religious liberty.[27] On the other hand, the papacy had no intention of giving up the church privileges gained in the previous century through Vatican diplomacy and skillful management of the legacy of the temporal power. Today in Italy, for example, there is still no law on religious freedom.

How did that change with Pope Francis? Francis has never spoken in general terms of the kind of legal and constitutional treatment Catholics should get, or look for, in a particular country. The legal and political framework of each church is very different, and Francis is very aware of that. Francis's ecclesiology is in favor of a Catholic Church free from the protections of the established church. He has spoken openly in favor of a secular state (in Italian, *stato laico*) and against nostalgia for the confessional state.[28]

Francis's ecclesiology is based on a practical ecclesiology of the theology of liberation and its attention to political praxis. Francis comes from a Latin American Catholicism that presupposes unity between church and people, and not only a mystical unity. The prophetic voice of Francis's Catholicism is part of post–Vatican II, late twentieth-century Christianity. It is a prophetic voice that is at once an insider, part of the system, and an outsider, critic of the system. It is an ambivalence that is also typical of Francis, and which Francis brought to the papacy in a way that is different from a similar ambivalence of all the post–Vatican II popes.

But if Francis is ambivalent, this is the same ambivalence of Vatican II and of *Gaudium et Spes*.[29] Francis is in no way nostalgic about the past when church and state were allied. It is noteworthy that in Italy Francis has gone against some of the old features of the established national Catholicism created by the concordat between Pius XI and the fascist regime of Benito Mussolini (updated in 1984 and still in force), and not only by asking forgiveness from the pentecostal churches persecuted under the fascists: he is the first pope to do that.[30] On more concrete and less historical issues, Francis invited church-owned businesses in Italy (such as the "religious hotels" in Rome) to pay taxes like other businesses; he started to clean up the Vatican Bank, one of the safe havens created in 1929 by the legal fiction that is the Vatican State; he advocated a more humane policy toward migrants and refugees, knowing that this will make Italy a state more multicultural and multireligious, so less Catholic.

The second factor is that Francis has a particular way of addressing political issues. The Jesuit Jorge Mario Bergoglio does not shy away from denouncing the injustices of our economic system, but he is very aware of the risks of the pope being manipulated by politicians (as has happened previously in Italy). Francis wants to keep politicians at arm's length, and he does nothing to hide that. On the other hand, what Francis is doing is trying to rehabilitate politics.[31] In doing so he is not advocating a revolutionary change, and certainly not a change whereby the public role of the church is less visible and less authoritative. For that matter, Francis's view of the church is not as liberal or radical as many credit him with. His is still a church that demands attention, respect, and a role in the public square. In other words, Francis's radicalism must not be mistaken for a political theology that advocates the radical end of some "established church" where it still exists.

What is relevant here is his perception of the signs of the times, and his ecclesiology in response to the signs of the times. This leads us to the third factor: Francis is a radical, social Catholic defending a way of life and a social system that is threatened by what in the encyclical *Laudato Si'* he called "the technocratic paradigm."[32] Francis is a progressive Catholic— progressive in the sense of a Catholic with no nostalgia for an idealized past. But he has, to be sure, an antimodern sensibility that is typical of Catholic thinkers of the 1930s (the decade Francis was born) such as Romano Guardini, whom he quotes more than once in *Laudato Si'*.

My contention here is that the reluctance of some progressive Catholics—like Pope Francis?—to get rid of the established church is connected to the role the church plays in the world of the "technocratic paradigm." We must ask ourselves if the established church is perhaps one of the few remaining bastions against the destruction of the welfare state, against "turbo capitalism," against the radical individualization of human life, and against neoimperialism and exceptionalism in the United States of America—a neoimperialism and exceptionalism where constantinianism has survived and survives disestablishment. It is not just about the amount of social work and welfare the church can provide with taxpayers' money allowed by the concordats. It is not merely about charities and philanthropic initiatives but also about the work that the government has outsourced to the churches, a long time ago in some cases, and that is now an integral part of the socioeconomic system.

This fear of the impact of the technocratic paradigm is a big factor. A radical withdrawal of the church from the public square would probably mean losing that pulpit that allows the Catholic Church to speak in favor and on behalf of those who are excluded from the economic system. In some contexts, the pulpit that allows the church to be present in the public square is equipped with privileges that we consider premodern (Catholic religion classes in public schools, tax exemptions for charitable initiatives, etc.), but it is also the last defense against the impact of the technocratic paradigm.

This reluctance to let go of that pulpit is not just one of the deep continuities between Francis and his predecessors; it is also one of the transversal issues that mark a clear difference between the Euro–Latin

American Catholicism of Francis and the Catholicism of the Anglo-Saxon world. In the Anglo-Saxon world, even the very idea of giving tax-payers' money to a church that opposes key elements of the capitalistic system would be perceived as ridiculous. There is also an ideological issue. In the Anglo-Saxon world political liberalism and theological liberalism are much more aligned and more overlapping than in Europe or anywhere else. This difference between the Euro–Latin American Catholicism of Francis and the Catholicism of the Anglo-Saxon world affects the kind of relationship Catholics have with the past (this includes constantinianism and the established church) and therefore their ideas about "church reform."

As important as the liberal/conservative divide is, the established church dilemma is one of the many examples of the redefinition of the rifts within global Catholicism. The importance of this is that in Francis there is a genuine ambivalence about the role of the church in the public square. His is a church that does not want to be politicized but reclaims its right and duty to be political, as is necessary for a prophetic church. This is not just ambivalence, but a dilemma that is caused by the profound changes in the role of the church in our globalized world.

THE "BRAVE NEW WORLD"
AND THE ESTABLISHED CHURCH

During the first half of the twentieth century the fight against constantinianism and the established church was about a Catholic Church that was still exclusive, in the sense that belonging to the Catholic Church defined the legal and social status of all members of the social and political community; at least this was the theory, though often less so in practice. To a large extent this remained the case in the immediate post–Vatican II period.

It seems to me that the new prophetic role of the churches in our time should lead us to ask new questions about, on the one hand, constantinianism and the imperial church and, on the other hand, the established church system. The Catholic Church of today—at least the church of Pope Francis—is much more inclusive, both theologically and in practice. It is no longer the church that signed the concordat with Mussolini in 1929, with Hitler in 1933, and with Franco in 1953.[33]

We are not in the 1930s, or in the 1950s, not even in the time of Vatican II. This chapter does not seek to argue for the maintenance of privileges for the Catholic Church or for other churches that still enjoy the special status granted them by concordats or similar juridical agreements with nation-states. Neither does it advocate new privileges in any way, shape, or form.

In choosing Francis as a name, Jorge Mario Bergoglio was surely aware that the early criticism against the constantinian church came from those "heretical movements" (to which early Franciscans were close) that saw in the gift of Constantine to the church a dangerous legacy.[34] The poor church that Francis advocates implies a reconsideration of the role of the church in the brave new world we live in, against the backdrop of the macro crisis of our time.

CONCLUSION

This chapter seeks to shine a light on the changed conditions surrounding the debate on the Christian, or better still, the Christ-like, character (Franz Overbeck called it *Christlichkeit*) of the established church as a legacy of the Constantinian age. The argument is that the great political, social, and economic changes in the world during the past fifty years require a new ecclesiological appraisal.

The churches today do indeed help many human beings survive the deep injustices of the neoliberal system. But the churches also build a substantial, if intangible and spiritual, alternative worldview. They do this thanks to a vast structure that made the church a partner of the empire (whatever we want to call it) and also a counter-empire. Both the imperial and counter-imperial souls of the church were built thanks to the alliance between two suspicious allies, Constantine and the church. It is also a legacy of the way that antagonistic alliance developed in the centuries afterward.

I have no intention here to romanticize the good old days of the established church. With the declaration on religious liberty, *Dignitatis Humanae* of Vatican II, the Catholic Church declared the end of the Constantinian age by giving up the idea of a "Catholic state." While expressing anguish over secularization, the magisterium of the Catholic

Church never reconsidered that fundamental step made by Vatican II. The "status quo ante" narrative that is the polemic against Vatican II can do nothing to resuscitate the confessional state.[35] The church has learned a great deal from the modern world about the theological need to acknowledge human rights, religious liberty above all. It still has something to learn.

The changed conditions in our world, and the changed roles between the church and states, more exactly between the church, the political authority, and non-state actors, could lead us to consider what can be let go of in the established church and what is worth retaining. In the process we will learn to understand better the role of the Catholic Church today in its historical and political complexity.

NOTES

For a more comprehensive treatment of the issues discussed in this chapter, see Massimo Faggioli, *Catholicism and Citizenship: Political Cultures of the Church in the Twenty-First Century* (Collegeville, MN: Liturgical Press, 2017; Italian ed. Rome: Armando Editore, 2018).

1. See on this Hervé Legrand, "Introduction: L'articulation entre annonce de l'Évangile, morale et législations civiles à l'ère post-constantinienne," in *Évangile, moralité et lois civiles: Gospel, Morality, and Civil Law,* ed. Joseph Famerée, Pierre Gisel, and Hervé Legrand (Zurich: LIT, 2016), esp. 23–34. See also Giuseppe Ruggieri, "Évangile, morale et lois civiles: Changements de paradigme," in *Évangile, moralité et lois civiles,* 167–84.

2. See Pope Francis's encyclical *Laudato Si'* (May 24, 2015), para. 109. For his view of "technocratic paradigm" and its impact on anthropocentrism, see paras. 101–36.

3. See Peter J. Leithart, who calls "root-and-branch rejection of 'Constantinianism' or 'Christendom' doubly wrong-headed" also because of the ongoing southern shift of global Christianity. Peter J. Leithart, *Defending Constantine: The Twilight of an Empire and the Dawn of Christendom* (Downers Grove, IL: IVP Academic, 2010), 12.

4. Gianmaria Zamagni, *Fine dell'era costantiniana: Retrospettiva genealogica di un concetto critico* (Bologna: Il Mulino, 2012), 11–19. See also the updated German edition, *Das "Ende des konstantinischen Zeitalters" und die Modelle aus der Geschichte für eine "Neue Christenheit": Eine religionsgeschichtliche Untersuchung* (Freiburg: Herder, 2016).

5. See Marie-Dominique Chenu, *Une école de théologie, le Saulchoir, avec les études de G. Alberigo, E. Fouilloux, J. Ladrière et J.-P. Jossua,* Preface by René Rémond (Paris: Cerf, 1985).

6. See Michel Fourcade, "Vatican II dans le débat théologico-politique français," in *La France et le Concile Vatican II*, ed. Bernard Barbiche and Christian Sorrel (Paris: Peter Lang, 2013), 101–26.

7. See Philippe Roy-Lysencourt, *Les Membres du Coetus Internationalis Patrum au Concile Vatican II. Inventaire des interventions et souscriptions des adhérents et sympathisants: Liste des signataires d'occasion et des théologiens* (Leuven: Maurits Sabbe Library, Faculty of Theology and Religious Studies—Peeters, 2014).

8. See Riccardo Burigana, "Progetto dogmatico del Vaticano II: La commissione teologica preparatoria (1960–1962)," in *Verso il concilio Vaticano II (1960–1962): Passaggi e problemi della preparazione conciliare*, ed. Giuseppe Alberigo and Alberto Melloni (Genoa: Marietti, 1993), 141–206, esp. 188–91.

9. See Silvia Scatena, *La fatica della libertà: L'elaborazione delle dichiarazione "Dignitatis humanae" sulla libertà religiosa del Vaticano II* (Bologna: Il Mulino, 2004), 21–42.

10. On *Gaudium et Spes*, see Yves Congar, "Église et monde dans la perspective de Vatican II," in *L'Église dans le monde de ce temps*, ed. Yves Congar and Michel Peuchmaurd (Paris: Cerf, 1967), vol. 3, 15–41, especially for the rupture with political Augustinianism and its subordination of the temporal order to the supernatural.

11. John XXIII, opening address of Vatican II, *Gaudet Mater Ecclesia* (October 11, 1962) (English translation in *The Documents of Vatican II*, ed. Walter M. Abbott [New York: Guild Press, 1966], 713). For a global interpretation of *Gaudet Mater Ecclesia*, see Giuseppe Alberigo, *Dalla laguna al Tevere: Angelo Giuseppe Roncalli da S. Marco a San Pietro* (Bologna: Il Mulino, 2000), 157–90.

12. See Massimo Faggioli, *John XXIII: The Medicine of Mercy* (Collegeville, MN: Liturgical Press, 2014), 99–102, with reference to Roncalli's diaries when he was patriarch of Venice (1953–58).

13. Vatican II, *Message to the World*, in *Acta Synodalia Sacrosancti Concilii Oecumenici Vaticani II*, cura et studio Archivi Concilii Oecumenici Vaticani, vols. 1–6 in 33 books (Vatican City: Typis Polyglottis Vaticanis, 1970–99), vol. I/1, 230–32.

14. See Massimo Faggioli, *Il vescovo e il concilio: Modello episcopale e aggiornamento al Vaticano II* (Bologna: Il Mulino, 2005), 401–2.

15. See Scatena, *La fatica della libertà*.

16. See Giovanni Turbanti, *Un concilio per il mondo moderno: La redazione della costituzione pastorale "Gaudium et Spes" del Vaticano II* (Bologna: Il Mulino, 2000); John W. O'Malley, *What Happened at Vatican II* (Cambridge, MA: Belknap Press of Harvard University Press, 2008), 265–66.

17. See Giovanni Turbanti, "Il ruolo del p. D. Chenu nell'elaborazione della costituzione *Gaudium et Spes*," in *Marie-Dominique Chenu: Moyen-Âge et modernité* (Paris: Le Saulchoir, 1997), 173–212.

18. The translation of conciliar texts used are those provided in Austin Flannery, OP, ed., *Vatican Council II: Constitutions, Decrees, Declarations* (Northport, NY:

Costello Publishing Company, 1996) (rev. ed., inclusive language). References are in the body of the text.

19. See, e.g., Loris Zanatta, *Del estado liberal a la nación católica: Iglesia y ejercito en los orígenes del peronismo 1930–1943* (Buenos Aires: Universidad Nacional de Quilmes, 1996).

20. "Message to Rulers," from "Final Messages of Vatican II, December 8, 1965," in Abbott, *The Documents of Vatican II*, 729–30.

21. See Alberto Melloni, *L'altra Roma: Politica e S. Sede durante il Concilio Vaticano II (1959–1965)* (Bologna: Il Mulino, 2000).

22. See Stephen R. Schloesser, "'Dancing on the Edge of the Volcano': Biopolitics and What Happened after Vatican II," in *From Vatican II to Pope Francis: Charting a Catholic Future*, ed. Paul Crowley, SJ (Maryknoll, NY: Orbis, 2014), 3–26.

23. See Wolfram Kaiser, *Christian Democracy and the Origins of European Union* (Cambridge: Cambridge University Press, 2011), 163–90.

24. The *Enchiridion dei Concordati: Due secoli di storia dei rapporti Chiesa–Stato* (Bologna: EDB, 2003) begins with the concordat between Pius VII and Napoleon (1801) and concludes with the agreements and concordats during the pontificate of John Paul II.

25. See also Joël-Benoît D'Onorio, ed., *La diplomatie de Jean Paul II* (Paris: Cerf, 2000).

26. See the May 6, 2016, speech Pope Francis gave in the Sala Regia in the Vatican on accepting the prestigious Charlemagne Prize: http://w2.vatican.va/content/francesco/en/speeches/2016/may/documents/papa-francesco_20160506_premio-carlo-magno.html.

27. See Samuel Huntington, *The Third Wave: Democratization in the Late Twentieth Century* (Norman: University of Oklahoma Press, 1991).

28. "States must be secular. Confessional states end badly. That goes against the grain of History. I believe that a version of laicity [English translation of the French *laïcité*] accompanied by a solid law guaranteeing religious freedom offers a framework for going forward. We are all equal as sons (and daughters) of God and with our personal dignity. However, everyone must have the freedom to externalize his or her own faith. If a Muslim woman wishes to wear a veil, she must be able to do so. Similarly, if a Catholic wishes to wear a cross. People must be free to profess their faith at the heart of their own culture not merely at its margins. The modest critique that I would address to France in this regard is that it exaggerates laicity. This arises from a way of considering religions as sub-cultures rather than as fully-fledged cultures in their own right. I fear that this approach, which is understandable as part of the heritage of the Enlightenment, continues to exist. France needs to take a step forward on this issue in order to accept that openness to transcendence is a right for everyone." Pope Francis, interview with the French Catholic magazine *La Croix*, May 16, 2016, www.la-croix.com/Religion/Pape/INTERVIEW-Pope-Francis-2016-05-17-1200760633 (English translation published in *Global*

Pulse Magazine, www.globalpulsemagazine.com/news/interview-with-pope-francis -by-la-croix/3184).

29. "It is very easy to slip unconsciously towards positions that may be associated with neo-Constantinianism or, on the contrary, towards positions that may be accused of naïve otherworldliness." Roberto Tucci, "La vie de la communauté politique," in Congar and Peuchmaurd, *L'Église dans le monde de ce temps*, vol. 2, 517.

30. See http://w2.vatican.va/content/francesco/en/speeches/2014/july /documents/papa-francesco_20140728_caserta-pastore-traettino.html. See also Raffaele Nogaro and Sergio Tanzarella, *Francesco e i pentecostali: L'ecumenismo del poliedro* (Trapani: Il Pozzo di Giacobbe, 2015).

31. See Diego Fares, "Papa Francesco e la politica," *Civiltà Cattolica*, no. 3976 (February 27, 2016): 373–86.

32. Pope Francis, *Laudato Si'* (May 24, 2015), para. 101 ff.

33. The concordat between Pius XII and Franco was abolished in 1980, after the dictatorship in Spain ended.

34. See Giuseppe Ruggieri, "Prefazione," in Zamagni, *Fine dell'era costantiniana*, 10.

35. For the survival of a Constantinian age mentality in the magisterial emphasis on "natural law," see Legrand, "Introduction: L'articulation entre annonce de l'Évangile, morale et législations civiles à l'ère post-constantinienne," 30–32.

SEVEN

"On Consulting the Faithful in Matters of Doctrine"

The Twenty-First Century

FÁINCHE RYAN

This chapter looks at another aspect of the journey since Vatican II: the important issue of the locus of authority in the church. For many centuries there was a prevailing view that the ecclesial body can be sharply bifurcated as *ecclesia docens*, on the one hand, and *ecclesia discens*, on the other. That is to say, in the ecclesial body teaching authority lies with those in ordained ministry, primarily with the episcopal and papal ministries. The rest of the ecclesial body has a more passive role. The majority belong to the *ecclesia discens*, the church that learns. In the context of this ecclesial understanding the documents of Vatican II introduced the concept of *sensus fidei* into the formal teaching of the church (*Lumen Gentium* 12 and 35). This development has led us into a period of contested authority. The way forward is still not clear. Locating authority in the church in a more theologically authentic manner is particularly relevant to the discernment of the social and political roles of the church. It is worth noting from the outset that the exploration of the locus of authority in the church is not isolated from similar explorations of authority in society.

In 1859 Cardinal Newman wrote an extended article titled "On Consulting the Faithful in Matters of Doctrine." This led him to be termed "the most dangerous man in England." This chapter begins with a review of the maelstrom of controversy that erupted around Newman and his argument against an exaggerated notion of *ecclesia docens*. It then turns to developments in the understanding of the locus of authority in Vatican II and subsequent theological exploration. The chapter concludes with a reflection on where we are now in Catholic tradition vis-à-vis the perspective of authority in the church.

CARDINAL NEWMAN: "ON CONSULTING THE FAITHFUL"

If a check be not placed on the laity of England they will be the rulers of the Catholic Church in England instead of the Holy See and the Episcopate. . . . [T]he laity are beginning to show the cloven hoof. . . . They are only putting into practice the doctrine taught by Dr Newman in his article in the *Rambler*. . . . What is the province of the laity? To hunt, to shoot, to entertain. These matters they understand, but to meddle with ecclesiastical matters they have no right at all, and this affair of Newman is a matter purely ecclesiastical. . . . Dr Newman is the most dangerous man in England, and you will see that he will make use of the laity against your Grace.[1]

Monsignor George Talbot (papal chamberlain to Pius IX, canon of St. Peters) wrote these words from Rome to Cardinal Manning, archbishop of Westminster, in April 1867,[2] ten years after the controversy about the role of the laity—the laity has no right to meddle in ecclesiastical matters—had erupted stemming from articles in a Catholic periodical, the *Rambler*.

The background to the article is significant. This is a very particular era in the history of the Catholic Church in England. Catholic emancipation is recent (1829). In the English Roman Catholic church at this time there are the recusant Catholic families, who had never converted to the established church, significant numbers of new emigrant Catholics (in particular, a large number of Irish emigrants), and, most significantly, the many converts from Anglicanism, of which Newman was one. In this setting the Catholic circle of the educated was small and intimate.

In 1848 an Oxford convert, J. M. Capes, had started the *Rambler*. It had a short run (1848–64), yet despite this and its relatively small circulation (800–1,000), it was an influential periodical. It played an important role in the history of English Catholicism during the nineteenth century. Initially the *Rambler* sought to limit its engagement to issues of politics, science, art, and literature. The circumstances of the time led it to increasingly engage in issues of Catholic education, which were perceived as having been left open to debate by church authorities, while seeking to avoid what it termed "technical theology." This opening of its field of concern led to friction with leading members of the newly established English hierarchy, in particular, with Cardinal Wiseman, the first archbishop of Westminster (1850–65), and Manning (cardinal, 1865–98). This was the context in which Newman composed his article "On Consulting the Faithful in Matters of Doctrine."

Newman is notable for having produced some of his best writings in situations where he felt obliged to defend himself against misinterpretation. This article in the *Rambler* is one of the best examples. The story begins with Augustine and Jansenism. Sir John Acton, coeditor of the *Rambler* (with Richard Simpson), remarked in a book review that Augustine "was also the father of Jansenism."[3] Rome had condemned Jansenism, and here is Acton linking Jansenism with the revered Augustine. There was much public reaction to this claim. Johann Joseph Ignaz von Döllinger (1799–1890) was persuaded to write a theological justification for this association of Jansenism with Augustine. The choice of Döllinger, noted for his resistance to the ultramontane claims of a centralized authority, was inevitably going to arouse the ire of members of the British hierarchy. They were becoming increasingly ultramontane, seeing Rome as the center of authority. Döllinger's theological response was published in the form of a letter in the December 1858 issue of the *Rambler*. Cardinal Wiseman was not impressed with Döllinger's piece, or with the *Rambler*.[4]

These actions led Acton to visit Newman for counsel. In a three-hour conversation, they discussed the matter. Acton described Newman as "most friendly" and was impressed by Newman's interest. Newman, while seeing value in the article, advised that henceforth the *Rambler*, a secular magazine run by untrained laymen, would do best to avoid theology and to side with ecclesial authority. He suggested this was strategically the best way forward for in this way, at the necessary time, the publication "will be able to plant a good blow at a fitting time with great effect. . . . Power, to be powerful, and strength, to be strong, must be exerted only now and then. It then would be strong and effective, and affect public opinion without offending piety or good sense."[5]

At this stage Newman's view is clear: while he saw the importance of the *Rambler* having a critical voice in public matters, untrained laymen should avoid theological comment. The *Rambler* was encountering problems because "it had treated of theology proper, it had done so in a magazine fashion, and it has allowed laymen to do so." This should not happen, for "it requires an explanation when a layman writes on theology."[6]

Trouble had not passed, however. In parallel with the Augustinian issue, problems were arising in the quite different field of Catholic education. In this field laypeople were also voicing their opinions. The January 1859 issue of the *Rambler* published an article by a leading government inspector of Catholic schools. While the author is unnamed, it was commonly known to have been written by Nasmyth Scott Stokes. The article criticized the bishops for "their sectarian refusal to co-operate with a Royal Commission into the state of primary education."[7] It argued that as Catholic primary schools received substantial financial state assistance, state inquiry was to be expected. Catholics should cooperate with the commission, open wide the doors of their schools, and show the richness of Catholic education, in particular, of their religious teaching. Stokes continued his argument in the February issue, warning of the dangers of Catholic isolation if grants were to be withdrawn and education standards to inevitably slip.

Another Catholic periodical, the *Tablet*, vehemently attacked the anonymous author of the article in the *Rambler* for encouraging disobedience to the bishops. Stokes's response was "that no episcopal decision had been made public, there had been no involvement of the laity, nor were faith and morals involved; the bishops could not object to the loyal expression of views which were irrefutable."[8] However, they could. It seems that on education matters also, authority resides with the hierarchy.

Döllinger's article, followed immediately by this implicit critique of bishops and Catholic schools, led to increased episcopal pressure on the *Rambler*. The key figure was Bishop Ullathorne (1850–88), the first bishop of Birmingham. This resulted in the editor, Simpson, stepping down. Newman agreed to step in, for a specified period—until the end of the year. Thus began his fateful association with the *Rambler*. Newman accepted editorship at this critical juncture reluctantly. He knew that the magazine appealed to many educated Catholics, and he was anxious that it continue. He perceived it as a "safety valve"[9] for the "laity" in their growing opposition to Wiseman and his policies. It was a matter of conscience for him to keep alive a work whose principles he agreed with: "the refinement, enlargement, and elevation of the intellect in the educated classes."[10] At the same time Newman sought to moderate what was perceived as the offensive tone of the *Rambler*.[11]

In the May edition, the first he edited, Newman commented on the bishops' recent pastorals on the Royal Commission on education. While apologizing for any offense inadvertently caused to the hierarchy by articles in the *Rambler*, he stated that, in his view, the bishops must "really desire to know the opinion of the laity on subjects in which the laity are especially concerned. If even in the preparation of a dogmatic definition the faithful are consulted, as lately in the instance of the Immaculate Conception, it is at least as natural to anticipate such an act of kind feeling and sympathy in great practical questions."[12] This reference to consultation of the laity was explosive. John Gillow, priest and professor at the Catholic seminary, Ushaw College, deemed this idea "virtually heretical."[13] It also evoked a response from Ullathorne. His concern was that the laity was being upset. The laity, he perceived, was a peaceable group, not wishing to hear of doubt. The word *consult* was the main issue. In Gillow's view Newman seemed to be implying that the infallibility of the church lay with the laity and not with the hierarchy. To this Newman responded, "To the unlearned reader the idea conveyed by 'consulting' is not necessarily that of asking an opinion. For instance, we speak of consulting a barometer about the weather. The barometer does not give us its opinion, but ascertains for us a fact. . . . I had not a dream of understanding the word in the sense of asking an opinion."[14]

This conciliatory move by Newman did not appease episcopal ire. Ulla-thorne suggested that Newman resign his editorship after the July issue. The editorship was to move to Acton.[15] This polemic led Newman to con-sider in theological depth the place of the laity in the church. He wrote "On Consulting the Faithful in Matters of Doctrine," published in the *Rambler* in July 1859. The article was published anonymously, but, again, everyone suspected that Newman was its author. This article was his first serious consideration of "Church," his first steps in Catholic ecclesiology. In his introduction to a 1961 republication of the article, John Coulson notes that "this work is fundamental not only to a fuller understanding of Newman's theory of doctrinal development, but to an appreciation of the importance he attaches to the laity in his theology."[16]

The article begins with a studied defense of the use of *consult* in the May 1859 piece. It proceeds to ask, "Why consult the laity?" It finishes with a lengthy exposition in which Newman outlined where he saw prece-dent for this method of being church, that is, the Arian controversy. This heresy of the fourth century had been studied intensely by the Anglican Newman. It had taught him that in the tradition the division between those teaching, *ecclesia docens*, and those taught, *ecclesia discens*, was not as clear-cut as contemporary standards wished to establish.[17]

Newman notes that the *Rambler* of May 1859 "has these words at p. 122: 'In the preparation of a dogmatic definition, the faithful are con-sulted, as lately in the instance of the Immaculate Conception.'"[18] As it is the little word *consult* that had proved so provocative, Newman first clari-fies his use of the term. In Latin the word has a stronger connotation, such as "to consult with" or "to take counsel," but for Newman, working with the English language, *consult* is "a word expressive of trust and deference, but not of submission." We consult a watch to ascertain the time. To consult is to inquire into a matter of fact. Newman carefully states that the writer of the article in May, himself, was not writing as a theologian for theologians but rather for a wider audience. The article cannot be read as implying that the advice, opinion, or judgment of laity was to be sought in reference to defining a doctrine, or teaching. Rather their belief is sought as "a testi-mony" to apostolic tradition on which any teaching is based. He goes on:

And, in like manner, I certainly understood the writer in the
Rambler to mean (and I think any lay reader might so understand

him) that the *fidelium sensus* and *consensus* is a branch of evidence which it is natural or necessary for the Church to regard and consult, before she proceeds to any definition, from its intrinsic cogency; and by consequence, that it ever has been so regarded and consulted. (55)

From Newman's point of view, the key point is that "the sense of the faithful is not left out of the question when it comes to defining doctrine" (56).

Why bring the laity into the discussion at all? The answer is obvious: "The body of the faithful is one of the witnesses to the fact of the tradition of revealed doctrine, and because their consensus through Christendom is the voice of the Infallible Church."[19] Newman continues:

I think I am right in saying that the tradition of the Apostles, committed to the whole Church in its various constituents and functions *per modum unius*, manifests itself variously at various times: sometimes by the mouth of the episcopacy, sometimes by the doctors, sometimes by the people, sometimes by liturgies, rites, ceremonies, and customs, by events, disputes, movements, and all those other phenomena which are comprised under the name of history. It follows that none of these channels of tradition may be treated with disrespect; granting at the same time fully, that the gift of discerning, discriminating, defining, promulgating, and enforcing any portion of that tradition resides solely in the *Ecclesia docens*.[20]

Newman concludes this section with words that might be said to begin the development of an ecclesiology that will be influential in the Second Vatican Council: "One man will lay more stress on one aspect of doctrine, another on another; for myself, I am accustomed to lay great stress on the *consensus fidelium*, and I will say how it has to come about."[21]

SENSUS FIDELIUM: THE CATHOLIC WITNESS

Newman explains that his interest in the *sensus fidelium* stems not from his Anglican tradition but from his interaction with the Jesuit theologian Giovanni Perrone, SJ (1794–1876), when he was in Rome (1846–47).

Newman saw in Perrone a developed theology of the *sensus fidelium*. Placing great emphasis on the *sensus fidelium* and its relation to the *sensus ecclesiae*, Perrone understood the *sensus fidelium* as helping to account for matters of Catholic dogma that lacked patristic testimony. Perrone spoke of the *sensus ecclesiae* that can be gathered from a double source, that is, from the manner in which both pastors and faithful conduct themselves.[22] Newman notes that Perrone not only joins together the *pastores* and *fideles*, but simultaneously contrasts them: the "faithful" do not include the "pastors."

Perrone uses many examples in his argumentation. At various times, and in relation to various doctrines, he speaks of the force of the *sensus fidelium* as distinct (not separate) from the teaching of their pastors. While the strongest power of proof lies in the "general agreement" of faithful and pastors, Perrone cites the Spanish Dominican Melchior Cano (1509–60) as teaching that "in a question of faith, the general agreement of the Faithful makes for a belief by no means light."[23] In addition, Perrone cites Petavius, a sixteenth-century French Jesuit, who in turn cites St. Paulinus: "Let us pay attention to the judgement of all the faithful, because the spirit of God breathes into every faithful—*quia in omnem fidelem Spiritus Dei spirat*."[24] All of this, for Newman, indicates a strong tradition bearing witness to the importance of paying attention to the common judgment of all the faithful.[25]

Toward the end of the article, it is with some irony that we find Newman write so fulsomely of his own contemporary episcopate that it can nearly do without the *sensus fidelium*, so wonderful and rich is this era: "As to the present, certainly, if there ever was an age which might dispense with the testimony of the faithful, and leave the maintenance of the truth to the pastors of the Church, it is the age in which we live. Never was the Episcopate of Christendom so devoted to the Holy See, so religious, so earnest in the discharge of its special duties, so little disposed to innovate, so superior to the temptation of theological sophistry."[26] Newman comments that perhaps this is the reason the *sensus fidelium* has fallen to the background. However, he then provides a balance by saying that each constituent part of the church has its proper function and cannot be safely neglected.

> I think certainly that the *Ecclesia docens* is more happy when she has such enthusiastic partisans about her . . . than when she cuts off the

faithful from the study of her divine doctrines and the sympathy of her divine contemplations, and requires from them a *fides implicita* in her word, which in the educated classes will terminate in indifference, and in the poorer in superstition.[27]

Indeed, important negotiations and communications must be constantly in play.

TWO ECCLESIOLOGIES OVERLAID: VATICAN II

It has been said that the distinctiveness of the council was the way in which the ordained leaders of the Catholic tradition engaged in a major self-assessment. Cardinal Kasper noted that the Second Vatican Council was the "first time a general council asked itself the question: Church, what are you? Church, what do you have to say for yourself?"[28] The issue with which Newman wrestled—the role of the faithful, the laity, in the church—was given real prominence in some of the texts. Yet alongside this, when it comes to the consideration of the role of the hierarchy, we find clear evidence of another model: a clear separation between *ecclesia docens* and *ecclesia discens*. In the texts of Vatican II there are two ecclesiologies and they overlay each other. One is an ecclesiology of inclusive sharing in the Body of Christ; the second is an ecclesiology that works with a division between *ecclesia docens* and *ecclesia discens*. These are juxtaposed, but never fully integrated.

Church as People of God and the *Sensus fidelium*

The seed planted by John Henry Newman, who, as we have seen, initiated a move away from a stark distinction between an active and a passive church, bore fruit in texts such as *Lumen Gentium* and *Dei Verbum*.[29] Yves Congar was another influential source. In his *Jalons pour une théologie du laïcat* (1954), which appeared three years later in translation as *Lay People in the Church*, he gave serious attention to the concept of *sensus fidelium*. Throughout history different terms have been used to express this belief—*sensus* or *consensus fidelium, sensus ecclesiae, sensus catholicus, sensus fidei, christiani populi fides, communis Ecclesiae fides* (as in Pius XII's

Munificentissimus Deus). The terms, while not exactly equivalent, suppose a common basis, which Congar formulates thus: "There is a gift of God (and of the Holy Spirit) which relates to the twofold reality, objective and subjective, of faith (*fides quae creditur, fides qua creditur*), which is given to the hierarchy and the whole body of the faithful together . . . and which ensures an indefectible faith to the Church."[30]

There are two key texts: *Lumen Gentium* 12 and *Dei Verbum* 8. In these documents, the theology of *sensus fidelium* was developed in the context of the recovery of the image of the church as People of God. The recovery of this image of the church enabled people to think creatively, to consider visions of co-responsibility, of collaboration. Church as People of God implies a certain equality, one might say a radical equality, rooted in our common baptism. It speaks of the priestly quality of an anointed people, making a pilgrimage in the world, through time, toward an eschatological conclusion, that is to say, toward a future way of being alive with Christ that is already sacramentally present. It is precisely this eschatological tension that makes it so important and so difficult to get a theology of the *sensus fidelium* right. The image of People of God articulates a vision of a church open to such change as will help in realizing the mission of proclaiming God's love to all in a plurality of world contexts and times. *Lumen Gentium* 12 makes explicit reference to the *sensus fidelium*:

> The holy people of God shares also in Christ's prophetic office; it spreads abroad a living witness to Him, especially by means of a life of faith and charity and by offering to God a sacrifice of praise, the tribute of lips which give praise to His name. The entire body of the faithful, anointed as they are by the Holy One, cannot err in matters of belief. They manifest this special property by means of the whole peoples' supernatural discernment in matters of faith [*hanc suam peculiarem mediante supernaturali sensu fidei totius populi manifestat*] when "from the Bishops down to the last of the lay faithful" they show universal agreement in matters of faith and morals [*universalem suum consensum de rebus fidei et morum exhibit*]. That discernment in matters of faith [*illo enim sensu fidei*] is aroused and sustained by the Spirit of truth. It is exercised under the guidance of the sacred teaching authority, in faithful and respectful obedience to which the people of God accepts [*vere accipit*] that which is not

just the word of men but truly the word of God. Through it, the people of God adheres unwaveringly [*indefectabiliter adhaeret*] to the faith given once and for all to the saints, penetrates it more deeply [*profundius penetrat*] with right thinking, and applies it more fully in its life [*in vita plenius applicat*].

In this passage it is clearly stated that the entire people of God, aroused by the Holy Spirit, is involved in the discernment of the faith. Four verbs—*accipit, adhaeret, penetrat, applicat* (accept, adhere, penetrate, apply)—are used to describe this process. The *sensus fidelium* is understood as a connatural sensitivity to what it is to be a Christian, an ability to "hear" Christ's voice as church, as People of God—to listen together.

Dei Verbum 8 speaks in like manner, although the terms "sensus fidei" and "consensus fidelium" are not explicitly deployed.

What was handed on by the apostles comprises everything that serves to make the people of God live their lives in holiness and increase their faith. In this way the Church, in its doctrine, life and worship, perpetuates and transmits to every generation all that it itself is, all that it believes.

This tradition which comes from the Apostles develops in the Church with the help of the Holy Spirit. For there is a growth in the understanding of the realities and the words which have been handed down [*crescit enim tam rerum quam verborum traditorum perceptio*]. This happens through the contemplation and study made by believers, who treasure these things in their hearts (see Luke 2:19, 51) through a penetrating understanding of the spiritual realities which they experience.

Here again there is an emphasis on the role of the whole body of the faithful in the transmission of the tradition.

Reading farther on in this passage we seem to see the evidence of another ecclesiology: the growth in spiritual insight that comes from the "intimate sense of the realities which they experience" comes also "from the preaching of those who, on succeeding to the office of bishop, have received the sure charism of truth" (*ex praeconio eorum qui cum episcopatus successione charisma veritatis certum acceperunt*). So, while the opening lines of *Dei Verbum* 8 indicate a move from the old idea of a teaching church and a listening church, it proceeds to remind us of those who "through Episcopal succession" have received "the sure gift [charism] of truth." This reference to the sure gift of truth (*veritatis certum*) in the episcopal ministry could be taken to mean that the bishops simply look to the laity for confirmation that what they are doing is correct. One thinks of Newman and his struggles with the word *consult*.

There is a similar tension in *Lumen Gentium*. *Lumen Gentium* 12 is in a chapter titled "The People of God" (ch. 2). *Lumen Gentium* 25 is in chapter 3, "On the Hierarchical Structure of the Church and in particular on the Episcopate." In this section of *Lumen Gentium* there is scant reference to the whole people of God. We read that bishops are

> authentic teachers, that is, teachers endowed with the authority of Christ, who preach to the people committed to them the faith they must believe and put into practice, and by the light of the Holy Spirit illustrate that faith. They bring forth from the treasury of Revelation new things and old, making it bear fruit and vigilantly warding off any errors that threaten their flock. . . . In matters of faith and morals, the bishops speak in the name of Christ and the faithful are to accept their teaching and adhere to it with a religious assent [*obsequio adhaerere debent*]. (*LG* 25)

Thus, in the same documents, sometimes even in the same section and paragraph, two distinct ecclesiologies seem to be knitted together. There is juxtaposition but no real integration. Despite the recovery of the image of the People of God as foundational, the understanding of the church as divided into an *ecclesia docens* and an *ecclesia discens* (teaching church and learning church) persists in the documents of Vatican II. In this vision of the church the hierarchy is credited with active infallibility; the infallibility of the "learning church" is regarded as merely passive. The *sensus fidelium* in this perspective ceases to function as a distinct theological source.

In sum, different visions of ecclesiology overlay one another in the documents of Vatican II. That is to say, an ecclesiology built on the narrative of the People of God overlays an older ecclesiology articulated in terms of an active *ecclesia docens* and a passive *ecclesia discens*. Clearly, with this unresolved tension the road ahead will require careful navigation, and negotiation. The question arises, who will negotiate, and who will navigate?

THE JOURNEY FROM VATICAN II:
NAVIGATING THE TENSIONS

How might the concept of *sensus fidelium* be better integrated into the life of the church? This question has received widespread attention from theologians in recent decades. The International Theological Commission decided to devote one of the three documents written during its five-year term (2009–14) to this theme. Published in 2014, the document was titled "*Sensus Fidei* in the Life of the Church."[31] In 2015 the Catholic Theological Society of America chose *sensus fidelium* as the theme for its annual convention. The following year, 2016, the Catholic Theological Association (U.K.) annual conference had the arresting title, "*Sensus Fidelium*: Listening for the Echo."[32]

In all these efforts one can see a threefold aim. The first is to clarify and develop the rich heritage of the importance of the *sensus fidei* in the life of the church and to develop this heritage in a theologically authentic way. Perhaps the most important development is the identification of the *sensus fidelium* as an authentic "locus theologicus." The second aim is to explore in what way the *sensus fidelium* could be given better expression institutionally. There is an emphasis in these documents on the need for renewed programs of formation in faith and new canonical structures of communication. Third, there is some initial exploration of how the workings of *sensus fidei* interact with public opinion in the church and in pluralist societies.

Sensus fidelium: The Heritage

The International Theological Commission document begins by giving attention to the first of these tasks. It provides an excellent overview of the history of the rich extant theological tradition pertaining to this concept. In the opening paragraphs, parameters and terms are clarified. The *sensus fidei* is described as both a personal capacity of the individual believing member of the church and a communal and ecclesial reality, "the instinct of faith of the Church herself" (3). This convergence (*consensus*) of the baptized, of the individual's *sensus fidei* and the *consensus fidelium*, we read, "is a sure criterion for determining whether a particular doctrine or practice belongs to the apostolic faith" (3). For clarity the authors of the document tell us that they will use the term *sensus fidei fidelis* to describe the personal capacity of the believer for discernment in matters of faith (*sensus fidei*). To refer to the ecclesial instinct of faith the term *sensus fidei fidelium* (*sensus fidelium*) will be used. The aim of the document is "to clarify and deepen some important aspects of this vital notion in order to respond to certain issues, particularly regarding how to identify the authentic *sensus fidei* in situations of controversy," for example, when there is tension between the teaching of the magisterium and "views claiming to express the *sensus fidei*" (6). The strong role attributed to the Holy Spirit active in the lives of all members of the church for the first five hundred years is emphasized. Newman is cited to remind us of the crucial role of the laity in the era of the great councils.

The critical role of the Second Vatican Council in reestablishing the importance of the *sensus fidei* in the life of the church is noted in the following passage:

> Banishing the caricature of an active hierarchy and a passive laity, and in particular the notion of a strict separation between the teaching Church (*Ecclesia docens*) and the learning Church (*Ecclesia discens*), the council taught that all the baptised participate in their own proper way in the three offices of Christ as prophet, priest and king. In particular, it taught that Christ fulfils his prophetic office not only by means of the hierarchy but also via the laity. (4)

However, as noted above, the council seems to both banish this strict separation and then effectively reestablish it, sometimes in the same paragraph.

On a second level, in recent theology the *sensus fidelium* begins to be identified as a *locus theologicus*. Thus at the 2015 Convention of the Catholic Theological Society of America John J. Burkhard directed attention to *Dei Verbum* 8, a pioneering passage, which he comments "makes clear that the *sensus fidei fidelium* is more than a static *locus theologicus* for the content of revelation."[33] In this it contrasts with the more static concept of *Lumen*

Gentium 12. *Dei Verbum* 8 emphasizes the dynamic character of revelation: the "*sensus fidei fidelium* is a living, dynamic deepening of the understanding of divine truth that proceeds throughout history as humankind (and the cosmos) moves towards its eschatological goal."[34]

Burkhard directs attention to the work of the German theologian Wolfgang Beinert. Beinert shows how the Second Vatican Council significantly expanded the notion of the *sensus fidei fidelium* as a *locus theologicus*.[35] He identifies four periods of development: first, when it was seen as a witness to the tradition; second, as an echo of what the magisterium taught; third, *sensus fidei fidelium* as a witness to church dogma when other sources were not available; and more recently, fourth, at Vatican II where the understanding seems to be emerging that "the *sensus fidei fidelium* not only witnesses to Christian truth but contributes to the emergence of that truth."[36] This last, that *sensus fidei fidelium* contributes to the emergence of truth, is a remarkable statement.[37]

Toward Ecclesial Expression of *Sensus fidelium*

There is clear recognition of the necessity of formation for the whole body of the church. The International Theological Commission document links the *sensus fidei fidelius* and the theological virtue of faith, understood as a form of knowledge based on love. Lived faith (*fides formata*) is the necessary root of the *sensus fidei fidelius* (57). Formation is identified as through prayer and liturgy, as well as by the reading of scripture. Significantly, though, the role of theology is minimized, even sidelined.

> Unlike theology, which can be described as *scientia fidei*, the *sensus fidei fidelis* is not a reflective knowledge of the mysteries of faith which deploys concepts and uses rational procedures to reach its conclusions. As its name (*sensus*) indicates, it is akin rather to a natural, immediate and spontaneous reaction, and comparable to a vital instinct or a sort of "flair" by which the believer clings spontaneously to what conforms to the truth of faith and shuns what is contrary to it. (54)[38]

This distinction is altogether too stark. Theology must necessarily have a role in the formation of the *sensus fidei fidelius* alongside, rather than distinct from, the "vital instinct" of the believer and the liturgical practices that form them.

This leads to another level of reform: the need for canonical reform. Beinert notes that for communion ecclesiology to successfully operate this vision must be "securely anchored in canon law. Individual gestures of goodwill or the toleration of privileges are not enough. There must be clarity regarding the structural and institutional elements which themselves need to be better explained. It must also not be forgotten that channels of communication must be established that admit the right of action from below toward the top."[39] This, he goes on to say, is not to call into question the hierarchical structure of the church but simply to seek (institutional) forms that are transparent and fruitful. The challenge for our time is how to give due force to an ecclesiology of equality in the Holy Spirit while at the same time validating the importance of the diversity of roles within the ecclesial body.

The need for structural reform can be clearly exemplified when we think of two vital issues in contemporary discussion of the ecclesia, namely, the role of the theologian and the role of women. The role of women is often simplified to an argument about rights and power, often centered on the issue of ordination. Locating the case for structural reform of the ecclesial role of women within this framework poses the danger that the hierarchy/laity, *ecclesia docens/ecclesia discens* way of being church will be perpetuated. We will have more hierarchy. The ecclesial issue is much deeper. It is a fundamental recognition that women as well as men are gifted, gifted equally and gifted diversely.

With regard to the role of the theologian in the *ecclesia*, we have had shocking examples of the abuse of institutions of hierarchical authority in recent decades: Jacques Dupuis and Elizabeth Johnson and many more unnamed, who have been silenced or disciplined without due process. The current structure and institutional arrangements in the church facilitate this abuse of authority. While institutional reform is often necessarily slow, there is now an urgency in these matters that cries out for attention. It is essential if the theologian is to contribute to the emergence of truth.

We all share in the one baptism. It is manifest that the *sensus fidei fidelium* is alert to this deep ecclesial reality. The challenge of today is how to give it appropriate expression. We are in a period of debate and discussion on a very wide front. What is critical is that we are allowed to debate, to disagree, to argue without the power structures of the *ecclesia* being wielded to control, to silence. As Timothy Radcliffe has noted:

> Being truthful takes time. The role of the *magisterium* is, or ought to be, to ensure that the Church takes the necessary time. It needs to pose tough questions when new views are articulated, not because of a fear of change or as "doctrinal enforcers" though that may sometimes be necessary but to ensure that in the search for truth we do not take lazy shortcuts and grab at premature and inadequate answers. The role of the *magisterium* is to keep us talking, thinking and praying about what is central to our faith, as we journey towards the one who is beyond all words.[40]

Sensus fidelium and Its Interaction with Public Opinion

An important task is the exploration of how *sensus fidelium* interacts with public opinion. In this regard the International Theological Commission document notes that "the *sensus fidei* gives an intuition as to the right way forward amid the uncertainties and ambiguities of history, and a capacity to listen discerningly to what human culture and the progress of the sciences are saying. It animates the life of faith and guides authentic Christian action" (70).

In contemporary democracies, public opinion is often taken as majority opinion, and often shaped by the media. In this regard it is important to note that the church is not structured according to the principles of a secular political society. This cannot be an adequate way of journeying toward the truth in the church. Writing in 1994, Cardinal Walter Kasper was happy to speak of the democratization of the church but noted this is not identical to the way of working of a democratic state. Rather in his view it seeks to describe

> something which is itself legitimate, namely a kind of democratic approach which includes among its points of reference the transparency of opinion-forming and decision-making and the joint participation of all involved. A positive atmosphere where open discussion and argument are possible can also be meant. However, if the democratisation of the Church is synonymous with the demand

that the various charisms, positions of office and modes of service become undifferentiated and uniform, then the theological greatness of the "People of God" has been confused with a more political greatness.[41]

The document of the International Theological Commission closes by citing from the 1971 document of the Pontifical Council for Social Communications, *Communio et Progressio*. The citation identifies the need for regular dialogue, for constant communication, and for good use of structures of consultation.

> Catholics should be fully aware of the real freedom to speak their minds which stems from a "feeling for the faith" and from love. It stems from that feeling for the faith which is aroused and nourished by the spirit of truth. . . . Those who exercise authority in the Church will take care to ensure that there is responsible exchange of freely held and expressed opinion among the People of God. More than this, they will set up norms and conditions for this to take place. (124)[42]

Institutional reform is necessarily slow. The whole church, the *sensus fidei* of the *sensus fidelium*, needs formation at a deep and profound level. The church needs to develop and practice new modes of listening. In this sense, reeducation in Catholic virtue is required. We need to learn afresh what it is to be church: *all are anointed with an invisible anointing*. These are the words of Thomas Aquinas in his commentary on Hebrews:

> To show Christ's excellence, he says that He was anointed with the oil of gladness. For He is a king. . . . He is also a priest: "You are a priest forever according to the order of Melchizedech" (Ps. 109:4). He was also a prophet. . . . It also befits Him to be anointed with the oil of holiness and gladness: for the sacraments, which are vessels of grace, were instituted by Him. . . . This anointing also befits Christians, for they are kings and priests: "You are a chosen race, a royal priesthood" (1 Pt. 2:9); "You have made us a kingdom and priests for our God" (Rev. 3:10). Furthermore, He has the Holy Spirit, Who is the spirit of prophecy: "I will pour out

my spirit upon all flesh; and your sons and your daughters shall prophesy" (Jl. 2:28).

Therefore, all are anointed with an invisible anointing: "Now he that has confirmed us with you in Christ and that has anointed us is God: who has also sealed us and given the pledge of the Spirit in our hearts" (2 Cor. 1:21); "But you have the unction from the Holy One and know all things" (1 Jn. 2:20).[43]

NOTES

1. John Henry Newman, *On Consulting the Faithful in Matters of Doctrine*, Introduction by John Coulson (London: Collins Liturgical Publications, 1961); reissued with a Foreword by Derek Worlock, Archbishop of Liverpool (London: Collins Liturgical Publications, 1986), 41. Subsequent citations refer to the 1986 reissue.

2. Ibid., 41.

3. Ibid., "Introduction," 4.

4. Ian Ker, *John Henry Newman: A Biography* (Oxford: Oxford University Press, 1988), 474.

5. Charles Stephen Dessain and Thomas Gornall, SJ, eds., *The Letters and Diaries of John Henry Newman*, vols. 1–6 (Oxford, 1978–84), vols. 11–22 (London, 1961–72), vols. 23–31 (Oxford, 1973–77). Quotation from vol. 18, Letter to Sir John Acton, December 31, 1558, 559–62 (quote on page 562).

6. Newman, *On Consulting the Faithful*, "Introduction," 6.

7. Ker, *John Henry Newman*, 474.

8. Ibid.

9. Dessain and Gornall, *Letters and Diaries of John Henry Newman*, vol. 19, 69.

10. Ker, *John Henry Newman*, 475.

11. Dessain and Gornall, *Letters and Diaries of John Henry Newman*, vol. 19, 76.

12. Ker, *John Henry Newman*, 478.

13. Roderick Strange, ed., *John Henry Newman: A Portrait in Letters* (Oxford: Oxford University Press, 2015), 315.

14. Dessain and Gornall, *Letters and Diaries of John Henry Newman*, vol. 19, 135.

15. It was at this time that Newman gave his oft-quoted response to Ullathorne's query, "Who are the laity?": "I answered (not these words) that the Church would look foolish without them." *On Consulting the Faithful*, "Introduction," 18, 19.

16. Ibid., 1.

17. Michael Slusser, in his article "Does Newman's 'On Consulting the Faithful in Matters of Doctrine' Rest upon a Mistake?," *Horizons* 20, no. 2 (1993): 234–40, disputes Newman's claim that during the Arian controversy Christian faith was

upheld more consistently by the faithful than by the leaders or bishops. This does not, however, take away from his rigorous thesis of the dogmatic importance of the *sensus fidelium*.

18. Newman, *On Consulting the Faithful*, 53, 54.

19. Ibid., 63.

20. Ibid.

21. Ibid.

22. "Es duplici fonte eum colligi posse arbitramur, tum scilicet ex pastorum tum ex fidelium sese gerendi ratione." Ibid., 65.

23. English translations of Newman's Latin are from the republished article in *Cross Currents* 2, no. 4 (1952): 69–97, at 76n6. Newman cites the Latin: "Præstantissimi theologi maximam probandi vim huic communi sensui inesse uno ore fatentur. Etenim Canus, 'In quæstione fidei,' inquit, 'communis fidelis populi sensus haud levem facit fidem'" (143). Newman, *On Consulting the Faithful*, 66.

24. "Ut de omnium fidelium ore pendeamus, quia in omnem fidelem Spiritus Dei spirat." Newman, *On Consulting the Faithful*, 68.

25. "Petavius speaks thus, as he quotes him [St. Paulinus]: '*Movet me, ut in eam [viz., piam] sententiam sim propensior, communis maximus sensus fidelium omnium.*' By '*movet me*' he [St. Paulinus] means, that he attends to what the *cœtus fidelium* says: this is certainly not passing over the fidèles, but making much of them." Newman, *On Consulting the Faithful*, 68.

26. Ibid., 103.

27. Ibid., 106.

28. In his article Walter Kasper describes how it was not until the fourteenth, fifteenth, and sixteenth centuries that the church began to reflect on its nature. The quarrels of the Reformation were very much concerned with an understanding of what the church is. In the nineteenth century, in the wake of Romanticism, Frederick Schleiermacher determined the direction of the Protestant church, while Johann Adam Möhler was influential on the Catholic side. For Catholics, though, it was Vatican II that gave serious attention to church identity issues. See Walter Kasper, "The Church as *Communio*," *New Blackfriars* 74 (1993): 232–44, at 232.

29. John J. Burkhard, "The *Sensus Fidelium*: Old Questions, New Challenges," *Proceedings of the Catholic Theological Society of America* 70 (2015): 27–43, at 28.

30. Y. M.-J. Congar, *Jalons pour une théologie du laïcat* (Paris: Cerf, 1953). English-language edition: *Lay People in the Church: A Study for a Theology of Laity*, rev. ed., trans. Donald Attwater (London: Fontana, 1964), 288.

31. International Theological Commission, "*Sensus Fidei* in the Life of the Church," 2014, www.vatican.va/roman_curia/congregations/cfaith/cti_documents /rc_cti_20140610_sensus-fidei_en.html. In the text, references to relevant paragraphs are from this source.

32. As an explanation for choosing this title, the Catholic Theological Association's website has the following statement: "After the First Vatican Council, John

Henry Newman hesitated before accepting what the Council had to say about papal infallibility. He was, said Lord Acton, 'waiting for the echo.' Acton understood, as many before and since have failed to do, that it is not the business of those whom we call 'teachers' in the Church to tell us things we did not know, but to articulate, interpret, clarify, the faith we have in common. Nothing can become 'the teaching of the Church' unless and until the People of God as a whole 'echo' the expression: react to it with something like 'Yes,' 'Amen,' 'that's it.'" www.ctagb.org.uk/id-2016 -sensus-fidelium.html. Proceedings of the conference are published in *New Black-friars* 98 (2017): 1074.

33. Burkhard, "Old Questions, New Challenges," 36. The International Theological Commission's "*Sensus Fidei* in the Life of the Church" notes the presence of the reality in the text; see nos. 46, 67, 87.

34. Burkhard, "Old Questions, New Challenges," 36.

35. See "Der Glaubenssinn der Gläubigen in Theologie und Dogmengeschichte: Ein Überblick," in *Der Glaubenssinn des Gottesvolkes: Konkurrent oder Partner des Lehramts?*, ed. Dietrich Wiederkehr (Freiburg: Herder, 1994), 66–131, at 87–109.

36. Burkhard, "Old Questions, New Challenges," 37.

37. The *sensus fidei fidelium* is "not only reactive but also proactive and interactive, as the Church and all of its members make their pilgrim way in history[,] . . . not only retrospective but also prospective, and, though less familiar, the prospective and proactive aspects of the *sensus fidei* are highly important. The *sensus fidei* gives an intuition as to the right way forward amid the uncertainties and ambiguities of history, and a capacity to listen discerningly to what human culture and the progress of the sciences are saying. It animates the life of faith and guides authentic Christian action" (70), International Theological Commission, 2014.

38. Here the International Theological Commission cites A. Möhler, *Symbolik*, §38: "Der göttliche Geist, welchem die Leitung und Belebung der Kirche anvertraut ist, wird in seiner Vereinigung mit dem menschlichen ein eigenthümlich christlicher Tact, ein tiefes, sicher führendes Gefühl, das, wie er in der Wahrheit steht, auch aller Wahrheit entgegenleitet."

39. Wolfgang Beinert, "Die Rezeptionsgeschehen in der Kirche," *Stimmen der Zeit* 214 (1996): 381–92, at 390–91. Translated and cited in Burkhard, "Old Questions, New Challenges," 34n18.

40. Timothy Radcliffe, "How to Discover What We Believe," *Tablet* (January 28, 2006): 13.

41. Kasper, "The Church as *Communio*," 238.

42. "Catholics should be fully aware of the real freedom to speak their minds which stems from a 'feeling for the faith' and from love. It stems from that feeling for the faith which is aroused and nourished by the spirit of truth in order that, under the guidance of the teaching Church which they accept with reverence, the People of God may cling unswervingly to the faith given to the early Church, with

true judgement penetrate its meaning more deeply, and apply it more fully in their lives. . . . Those who exercise authority in the Church will take care to ensure that there is responsible exchange of freely held and expressed opinion among the People of God. More than this, they will set up norms and conditions for this to take place" (116). "There is an enormous area where members of the Church can express their views on domestic issues. It must be taken that the truths of the faith express the essence of the Church and therefore do not leave room for arbitrary interpretations" (117). www.vatican.va/roman_curia/pontifical_councils/pccs/documents/rc_pc _pccs_doc_23051971_communio_en.html#Nota%2054; accessed April 28, 2016.

43. Hebrews 1:8, 9 [64] reflects patristic thinking. See also Laurence Ryan, "Patristic Teaching on the Priesthood of the Faithful," *Irish Theological Quarterly* (1962): 25–51, at 29.

EIGHT

The Secular Is Not Scary

PATRICK RIORDAN, SJ

The argument presented in this chapter is built around two authors whose works challenge standard readings of two classics of political philosophy: Augustine and his *City of God* and Jean-Jacques Rousseau and his *Le Contrat social.* The revisionist authors are the Australian theologian, Brian T. Trainor, interpreting Augustine, and the Canadian political scientist, Ronald Beiner, revisiting Rousseau. First Beiner on Rousseau is presented and discussed, then Trainor on Augustine.[1] The secular-religious tension is rooted in disputes about sovereign authority, and so, in the third section, there is an examination of how the understanding of sovereignty has changed. The fourth section identifies in secular debates echoes of the theological distinction of forms of the secular as advocated by Trainor. This leads to a conclusion in favor of a positive regard on the part of people of faith (the church) toward the secular in a modern pluralist society.

ROUSSEAU ON CIVIL RELIGION

Ronald Beiner in his monumental 2011 book, *Civil Religion: A Dialogue in the History of Political Philosophy*, traces the notion of civil religion throughout the Western philosophical corpus. Without religious commitment or affiliation himself, he examines how religion appears to the thinkers who have imagined a more rational world. With a primary concern for the political, this tradition of thought tends to see religion as a source of problems and so something to be controlled or managed from the perspective of the political. The range of authors surveyed is impressive, with Machiavelli, Hobbes, and Rousseau taken as principal advocates of a civil religion project.

The title of this chapter, "The Secular Is Not Scary," mirrors the shared opinion of those political thinkers for whom religion appeared scary because of the perceived threats of religious domination. Those thinkers who wanted to construct a state free from the control of the church struggled against an established acceptance of the legitimacy of a preeminent ecclesiastical authority. Political authorities that relied on coercion to effect obedience could be undermined by religious doctrines that taught a fear of punishments more dreadful than what the state could devise. Christ's words in Matthew's gospel, "Do not fear those who kill the body but cannot kill the soul; rather fear him who can destroy both soul and body in hell [*Gehenna*]" (Matt. 10:28), were seen as a direct challenge to the sovereign's ability to control by fear. The context is Christ's foretelling of the persecutions that will be suffered by his disciples, who will be delivered up to councils and governors and kings (Matt. 10:16–23). "Have no fear of them" (Matt. 10:26), is the advice that Jesus gives. Can a political authority that relies on fear tolerate such dismissive attitudes toward its threats and claims?

Must a political power rely on fear? Machiavelli raised the question explicitly when he asked whether it was better for the prince to be loved or to be feared. One might dispense with love, Machiavelli thought, but fear of the prince was essential for his effective rule.[2] Thomas Hobbes built his understanding of political reality on the motivating force of fear.[3] In the absence of a shared view of the good and a common commitment to realizing it, the only way in which diverse individuals each motivated to pursue their own interests could be made to conform to a common rule, he thought, was to bind them with fear, fear of the sovereign's power to punish and fear of the consequences of the absence of such power. Because he was so aware of the motivating force of fear, he was particularly concerned about the impact of religious belief on the stability and security of a commonwealth. A populace more in fear of divine retribution than of the magistrate's sword could not be relied on to obey. Hobbes defined religion in terms of fear: "Fear of power invisible, feigned by the mind, or imagined from tales publicly allowed."[4] Such fear was in direct competition with fear of visible powers, fear of the sovereign and its agents. Consequently, Hobbes laid down very strict conditions for the licensing of preachers and clergy within the commonwealth, so as to ensure that the effect of their ministry would be to support rather than jeopardize the power of the sovereign.

The emergence of the nation-state in European history can be interpreted against this background of an insecure political order needing to establish itself over against a religious world that claimed a higher authority. The creation of states each with its own claim to sovereignty meant rejection of any higher instance, and of course the Catholic Church was in both political and religious terms the target claimant to be rejected. William Cavanaugh has analyzed the myth of religious violence, and he has exposed the deception in the comforting story that the liberal state is the solution to the problem of violence.[5] What is really at stake is the attempt of political authority to claim for itself ultimate authority. The birth of the modern state was violent, to the extent that it involved the challenge to and destruction of a shared culture in which a higher authority than that of the civil ruler was recognized. The Westphalian solution to the political crises occasioned by the Reformation, formulated famously in the motto *Cuius regio, eius religio*, usually presented as the clever solution to the problem of religious violence, is actually the expression of the dominance of secular rulers over the church. This historical process resulted in the redefinition of religion, in such a way as to cater to the interests of a state that wanted to be seen as superior in its authority to that of the church. According to Cavanaugh, "The concept of religion being born here is one of domesticated belief systems which are, insofar as it is possible, to be manipulated by the sovereign for the benefit of the state."[6] He writes:

> The wars of religion were not the events that necessitated the birth
> of the modern state; they were in fact themselves the birth pangs of

the state. These wars . . . were fought largely for the aggrandizement of the emerging state over the decaying remnants of the medieval ecclesial order. It is not merely that political and economic factors played a central role in these wars, nor are we justified in making a facile reduction of religion to more mundane concerns. Rather, to call these conflicts "Wars of Religion" is an anachronism, for what was at issue in these wars was the very creation of religion as a set of privately held beliefs without direct political relevance. The creation of religion was necessitated by the new state's need to secure absolute sovereignty over its subjects.[7]

Although religion had been viewed from the political perspective primarily as a threat, it was also acknowledged to provide many benefits of a social and political nature. It was recognized as a powerful motivator and unifier of masses of people. And so Hobbes in the third part of *Leviathan* recommends how these positive benefits might be secured by the incorporation of religion in the life of the commonwealth. Similarly, Rousseau in the *Social Contract* also addresses this question and explores the possibility of creating and fostering a civil religion in the republic for the benefits that such religion might ensure for the peace and stability of the community.[8] The standard interpretation of Rousseau is that he in fact advocated a civil religion to deliver these benefits of motivation and cohesion while being under the control of the republic. The achievement of Ronald Beiner is to call into question this received interpretation.

Beiner provides a fresh critical reading of Rousseau on civil religion, revealing that the standard account is a misrepresentation. Far from concluding that politics can successfully instrumentalize religion for its purposes, as is usually thought to be his view, Rousseau came to the conclusion that the kind of religion that might be made useful for politics would not succeed because it would be severely deficient precisely as religion. Beiner points to Rousseau's survey of the various forms of religion linked to politics in book IV, chapter 8, of *The Social Contract* and remarks how he rejected all these forms of national religion. Rousseau then ends up with a form of toleration similar to that of Locke, but for Beiner this suggests Rousseau's own dissatisfaction with the form of civic-republican utopia that he had been developing. Beiner comments, "Rousseau's thought fluctuates between two opposed and contradictory standpoints, the standpoint of cosmopolitan brotherhood and the stand-point of national particularism, and the idea of civil religion seems to get caught in the interstices of this tension."[9] Beiner summarizes the argument as he finds it in Rousseau.

> Theocracy "works" as a civil religion but violates political right, whereas Christianity satisfies principles of moral legitimacy but does not "work" as a basis for politics. Good politics presupposes a false and inhuman religion; a true religion breeds bad politics. Hence each serves merely to cancel the practical validity of the other. If the problem of civil religion presents as much of an *aporia* as our reading has suggested, then one is required to reread the whole of the *Social Contract* in the light of this impasse with which the book concludes. True politics is particularistic and true religion is universalistic, and so "civil religion" does not name a genuine synthesis of religion and politics but rather identifies their necessary contradiction.[10]

REREADING AUGUSTINE

In a series of articles published in the *Heythrop Journal* as well as in his book *Christ, Society and the State*, the Australian theologian Brian T. Trainor offers a challenging interpretation of Augustine on politics that has obliged me to revise my acceptance of the standard reception at least among political philosophers. Crudely put, there is a reading of Augustine that sees him as anticipating Hobbes in understanding political power as the control of the destructive forces rooted in the human heart (*libido dominandi*) by the mastery of those same destructive forces monopolized by the sovereign. The standard reading is based on Augustine's use of two possible definitions of a political community, one of which he showed to be inapplicable to Rome, and so he supposedly abandoned it in favor of the alternative. On the definition of a political community as an association of reasonable beings united in commitment to justice and the common good Augustine could argue that it was not justice that had animated Rome's ambition but on the contrary a desire to dominate and exploit others that had led to a history of sedition and wars, both external and civil. As a Roman rhetorician, Augustine could not be content with a total dismissal of Rome's claims, and so he adopted an alternative definition that allowed Rome to qualify as a republic but that equally permitted the exposure of the empire as morally bankrupt.[11] This second definition focuses on the political community as an association of rational beings united in the love of common interests. With this alternative definition he could then distinguish the two cities that were polar opposites of each other: the City of God, as the community of those united in the love of God, and the earthly city, as the community of those who have in common the pursuit of self-interest and glory, a common interest that of its nature is contrary to unity.

Commentators on Augustine debate whether or not the change of definition requires him to abandon the emphasis on justice as a defining element of a city. Oliver O'Donovan classifies the reactions as either "idealist" or "realist."[12] Idealists want to stress that Augustine continues to hold the view that the true republic to be just must be Christian, or at least monotheistic, and committed to serving and implementing the will of God. A commonwealth united in love of its preferred objects would be a city only in name or appearance, not in reality. Realists, on the other hand, according to O'Donovan, see in Augustine's shift of emphasis an anticipation of the later modern understanding of the liberal polity as accommodating diverse comprehensive doctrines and welcome it accordingly.[13] Trainor takes a typically Catholic "both-and" stance, recognizing the novelty of the shift to a more open definition, without assuming the other understanding was abandoned. His task then is to explain how the two conceptions, idealist and realist, can be combined in a coherent understanding of the political entity. He attempts this by presenting Augustine's thought in such a way that the different distinctions and their coherence emerge.[14]

For Augustine, a well-ordered city is one in which God's will is observed and the divinely intended order prevails. However, even for a city that would want to achieve this ideal, it is not possible in history given the condition of human fallenness and sin. But in history there are different kinds of cities: those that strive in various degrees to be well ordered in the sense of giving each her due and those for which justice is irrelevant. Trainor uses the convenient images of "facing toward" and "facing away from" the divine order. The cities that face away from God, he suggests, are not on the scale of best-better-good-poor but are "to be characterised as unjust/unrighteous, as beyond the sphere of the truly ethical/just, rather than as inadequate in light of the ideal."[15]

With this complexity, then, we are not dealing simply with a two-term pair, "sacred" and "secular." The secular for Augustine is not a univocal category but comprises a range of stances that may be distinguished between those that are facing toward God—we might say more neutrally, open to the transcendent—and those that are facing away from him. Among those open to the transcendent are a great range of specimens depending on how well they incorporate values and virtues. However, they recognize that they are in progress toward an end, which may only be inchoately and vaguely known. Trainor uses the term "heuristic" in this context without elaborating on it. However, insofar as the common good is that end striven for (which may be understood as God as the highest good, or as the Good, simply, or as the human fulfillment of each and of all persons, in the language of *Mater et Magistra* and *Gaudium et Spes*), it might be named but will not be fully comprehended.[16] All these forms of regimes that face God realize justice in some degree, but in history and given human sinfulness their realization will be always incomplete relative to the justice of the City of God.[17] But even so, they can be understood in terms of both definitions offered, as a multitude united in a common view of what is just and a community united in love of some good. In proportion as the good loved is superior or inferior in the hierarchy of good, so will the corresponding community be better or worse.[18] Secular is not distinguished from religious, necessarily, in Trainor's reading of Augustine. He is attempting to explain how Augustine's two definitions of "city" (justice and interests) might be compatible and jointly applicable to some cities in history but not to all. That the members of the city are united in their pursuit of temporal and earthly goods (peace, justice, material well-being) does not preclude their being united also in doing the kind of justice that is prepared to give God what is due to God.

Some political communities are turned away from God, and they too can be labeled secular. At the extreme are cities whose existential orientation is away from the fullness of being and toward the abyss. The good they pursue, perhaps power, domination over others, accumulation of wealth without regard for the needs or well-being of others, occupies the position of "highest good" for them and so is equivalent to an idol, or false god. For such cities their injustice is absolute, in contrast to the relative justice of other polities facing the other way. This is an analytic device. It remains a question whether any such city could possibly exist, namely, one in which there is no redeeming good present, in which the natural virtues of prudence, justice, fortitude, and temperance are completely absent. Doubtless there are and have been in history regimes in which the whole political and legal order is based on crime. The regimes responsible for the Holocaust (Nazi Germany), the gulag (the Soviet Union), genocide (Rwanda), and the killing fields of Cambodia (Pol Pot) spring to mind as possible candidates.

Many of Augustine's commentators have wanted to read him as generalizing this form of the secular as applicable to all political communities in history. Hence they have seen in him an anticipation of the stance of Thomas Hobbes and more recent realist theorists. In their cases the label "secular" is to be understood, Trainor notes, as meaning "*only* secular," or "secular *against* the sacred,"or "intrinsically secular." But this reduction is false to Augustine's texts and his understanding of the city in history.

Trainor's point is summarized in the slogan "sacred reign—secular rule." Where the political authorities know themselves to be subordinate to higher standards that they do not set themselves, then they acknowledge the limitations of their sovereignty. These higher standards are operative in citizens' expectations that their governments and legislatures will make and apply laws and directives that deliver justice and serve the common good. Such expectations are consistent with a "knowing ignorance," an inability to say what exactly justice requires while recognizing injustice where it occurs. Consequently, the exercise of rule in the presence of higher claims does not necessarily mean the enactment of revealed prescriptions from Sacred Scripture. Trainor makes the point by contrasting his view of the Augustinian secular state with a theocratic state. Where the Augustinian regime is summarized as "sacred reign—secular rule," the theocratic state is summarized as "sacred reign—sacred rule." The possible inclusion of religiously sourced law in the law of the state would be decided solely by the secular authorities in an Augustinian earthly city, while in a theocratic state the religious authorities would decide. It is not difficult to imagine examples. Martin Luther King Jr.'s campaign for civil rights, campaigns to have conscientious objection recognized, and campaigns for reform of penal policy have all been religiously motivated but were successfully accepted for secular reasons. The changes were made by secular authorities, not by the religious authorities for religious reasons. Yet the human, secular, reasons for the changes in law were such that they were open to the higher, more ultimate reality: human dignity, justice, solidarity of humankind, and divine mercy.

A good example of this is the reliance on the assertion of the dignity of the human person, a dignity that remains undefined, for grounding the human rights articulated in the international covenants. The Universal Declaration of Human Rights as well as the Charter of the United Nations mention dignity in association with rights, but it is in the covenants that the claim is made explicitly for dignity as the ground of rights.[19] The notion of dignity is deliberately left vague. The drafters wanted to avoid invoking any particular religious doctrine even if they personally understood the claim of dignity in theological terms.[20] But the rich, vague language of dignity can function as a heuristic device allowing endorsement from many different perspectives, without having to adopt one of them.[21] This also provides a good example of what John Rawls has formulated as an overlapping consensus between comprehensive doctrines.[22] From within the political horizon of the overlapping consensus the officials of government can admit the existence of religions and churches and can accept also the importance of maintaining such a regime of secular governance as can merit the support of religious adherents, without allowing any one (or group) of them to dominate as the source of directives or legislation. "Sacred reign—secular rule" is clearly not to be "sacred reign—sacred rule."

Augustine's thought is complex, and has suffered from the tendency to simplify in order to make it accessible. To be secular does not require being turned away from God. Trainor insists that the Augustinian view of secularity requires a "firm distinction in principle between religious law and state law. Church and state are properly distinguished and 'separated' when it is publicly acknowledged that what aspects if any of religious law are to be enshrined in state law is a matter for secular authorities alone to determine."[23]

THE SECULAR TODAY: THE ISSUE OF SOVEREIGNTY

With this awareness of the ambiguity of "secular" we can see that the self-understanding of the modern state as the highest authority, subject to no higher authority—concretely from Westphalia, not to be subject to religious authority—has changed through history. The development of three features of modern statehood has considerably modified that sense of the state's sovereignty as absolute. These are linked but nonetheless distinguishable. Perhaps the most important one for my purposes has been the emergence and development of human rights as setting the standards below which no state should fall in the treatment of its own citizens. Articulated in the Universal Declaration of Human Rights (UDHR), they have become institutionalized in international law through the series of conventions that are in effect treaties between sovereign states, which willingly cede something of their sovereignty. Also, there are the thematic International Conventions, on Children's Rights, on Refugees, on Genocide.

A second related development has been the dissolution of the absoluteness of the principle of nonintervention. When a state evidently and systematically and seriously violates the human rights of its own people, then other states with UN backing are warranted in intervening militarily to stop the abuse. This has been invoked already in the twentieth century but is still very much disputed, given the difficulties of drawing lines. For instance, the apparent endorsement of a human right to democracy, which if acknowledged would allow states to intervene for the purposes of regime change in a state that denied its people their rights to democracy, has stimulated a lively debate. John Rawls's *Law of Peoples* can be read as developing a theory of international relations that, while taking human rights seriously, does not require or excuse military intervention to bring about democracy or the adoption of liberal values.[24]

The third development is the emergence of different forms of alliances between sovereign states. Our local case is the European Union, in which the states of Europe have pooled their sovereignty (Brexit campaigners interpret the sovereign decisions of the British Parliament as an abandonment of sovereignty instead of as a pooling of sovereignty with neighbors). There are other examples of such sovereignty pooling, and none provides as yet a clear example of resounding success. The different models are accommodations to local circumstances, whether we look at the ASEAN community, the Organization of African Unity, or the Arab League. What we can observe from these developments is the recognition by sovereign states in different environments that their sovereignty is in fact constrained, and if they wish to pursue goals of security, development, and welfare, they cannot do it alone but depend on the cooperation and contributions of neighbors. Thus they voluntarily cede some of their sovereignty to be bound by obligations that they freely take on. The motivating reason for accepting such obligations is the acknowledgment of a common good beyond a narrow self-interest consistent with independent action.

With these three developments there is a very significant shift in the meaning of sovereignty for the nation-state. It can no longer understand itself simply as the highest authority in its sphere, subject to none higher. Commitments and obligations arise from the full range of treaties and associations, so that states willingly take on the associated moral and legal constraints (while participating in the revision and amendment of the same). In the case of human rights legislation the higher authority to which states subject themselves is a moral one. It is not simply being bound by the threat of punishment (fear as the motivator), sanctions of one kind or another, even up to the point of military humanitarian intervention, as specified in the legal instruments. It is the endorsement of the statements of the UDHR and the conventions on human dignity, and the inviolability of human persons, and the treatment that is owed to them by virtue of simply being human. It is the acceptance that discrimination on the basis of race, religion, gender, or political allegiance is inappropriate for the dealings of a state with its own people. We should not underestimate the enormity of the achievement in sovereign nation-states agreeing to subject themselves to such higher standards. It should be read as progress from a negative stance of denial of any higher authority to a positive stance of recognition of the value and appropriateness of acknowledging some higher authority. This point does not warrant the conclusion, as some might be tempted to make, that this is a step toward recognizing the church (or religion in general) as a higher authority to which the state must subject itself.

On this point overoptimism should be avoided. In our world there is one significant state that, while it has pioneered the way for many other states to achieve freedom and the autonomy of self-government, remains a reluctant partner in international cooperation. The United States of America is not a state like any other, being more like an empire, and yet it continues to rely on the rhetoric of the sovereign nation-state.[25] Asserting its own sovereignty, it refuses to be subject to the jurisdiction of the International Criminal Court and is frequently an unwilling partner in the United Nations.[26] It is willing to cooperate where it can be in the leadership role, understandably so, wherever it is expected to be the paymaster of projects undertaken. The ambivalence of the United States in relation to human rights and military activity such as humanitarian intervention or preventive war has become public in debates in recent decades in which the standards the United States has set for itself are different from those it expects to be binding for the rest of the world.[27] But even allowing for such reservations, we have in these emerging institutions a development of the understanding of sovereignty, which is based less on denial of higher authority and now much more on a positive acknowledgment of shared interests along with shared moral standards that provide a horizon of common goods.[28] Augustine's contrasted explanatory concepts of justice and interests are in fact combined in the contemporary emergent self-understanding of the secular.

Had Rousseau already anticipated this learning curve that has been part of the self-discovery of the sovereign nation-state? Rousseau imagined a solution to the problems of freedom and equality in a republic in which the People is sovereign and the General Will is the source of all law and morality.[29] Seeing religion as threat but at the same time as a significant source of cohesion and motivation for a common project, he argued for the incorporation of religion within the polity as civil religion. Under the control of the General Will the civil religion might contribute to the unity of the People and underwrite the commitment of individuals to forgo the demands of their particular wills and subscribe to the common good. Rousseau realized, however, that the civil religion he imagined could not function as he wished, because it would lack the qualities of "true religion." As Beiner has shown us, Rousseau's survey of the forms of religion that might suit his purposes led to the conclusion that only the religion of the gospel might work, that is, one whereby no church set itself as competitor to the state. From within the horizon of the political at least in Rousseau's terms, a measure of autonomy for the state must be preserved while the state at the same time must recognize its own limitations, including the inability to control and instrumentalize religion.

SECULARISM IN CONTEMPORARY DEBATE

Trainor writes as a theologian in presenting his interpretation of Augustine on the secular. But could his distinction between the two forms of secularism be accessible from within the secular domain when reformulated in secular terms? I suggest that we find a parallel distinction between liberal and illiberal secularism operative in secular debates about the secular. This distinction relies on the linked value of liberalism. Liberal secularism is tolerant of a wide range of possibilities for individuals and groups to exercise their liberty and is compatible with a pluralist society; illiberal secularism, by contrast, espouses a worldview and is intolerant of worldviews at odds with itself. Illiberal secularism is typically antireligious. As a comprehensive doctrine in Rawls's sense, illiberal secularism is hegemonic, and hence unreasonable, being unwilling to accommodate other reasonable comprehensive doctrines while at the same time claiming (explicitly or implicitly) to provide the neutral meeting ground in which all can express their views. It is for this reason that Rawls includes secularism as one possible comprehensive doctrine and denies it can fulfill the role of providing the content of the overlapping consensus.[30]

In current debates within political philosophy, jurisprudence, and sociology we find a distinction between different forms of secularism that is in parallel to the distinction that Trainor argued for theologically. A brief survey of these debates is now offered. As Trainor underlines when contrasting his preferred model with theocracy, secular rule means that only appropriate secular reasons may be given for laws and policies. In a theocracy, by contrast, rule itself is sacred, and the laws and policies of government are derived from religious sources. Cécile Laborde has argued—sometimes against religious critics of secularism—for a defensible account of secularism that is both philosophically robust and politically viable. She defends a minimalist deflationary theory of secularism as a restraint on the reasons that might be invoked by states and their officials in justification of policy decisions. At its core is a norm of nonimposition (NIN), to the effect that a state may not rely on religious reasons in support of legislation. It would be wrong to expect citizens in a pluralist society to accept reasons that can hold no weight for them.[31] She calls this a deflationary account of secularism, wanting to contrast it with those versions of secularism that present it as a comprehensive doctrine or a substantive project for the conduct of states. She distances herself from such substantive positions that would see secularism as antireligious, and from supporters of secularism who look to it for the grounding of fundamental political values such as human dignity, equality, rights, or freedoms. Distinguishing the domains of opinion forming and decision making, justificatory secularism demands that decisions be justified using only nonreligious language, but opinions can be influenced and formed using any possible language, with images and values rooted in a speaker's worldview. As she puts it, the state is secular so that citizens don't have to be secular.[32]

She further distinguishes the stance of justificatory secularism from a similar line adopted by John Rawls in *Political Liberalism* and in later publications that the requirements and constraints of public reason apply also to citizens when they engage in the public sphere.[33] Just as officials of the state and judges of courts, citizens are expected on the Rawlsian account to use only reasons that are accessible to all participants in a pluralist context. Even if Rawls had later modified this requirement by adding a proviso, to the effect that religious language might be used in public debate on the condition that it is translated into reasons that are acceptable to all, his position maintained a high demand on what is permissible in public speech.[34] Laborde finds this excessive, arguing that while the state is required to be secular in its justification of its policies, there is no reason to demand the same stance from citizens. In this she joins other critics of Rawlsian liberalism who see it as making too many concessions to secularism in its illiberal form.[35]

Justificatory secularism is of value and interest to citizens of religious conviction, because it both protects them from having imposed on them religious perspectives alien to their own convictions and provides them with the guaranteed freedoms of conscience and speech that will enable them to take part in public life and debate on the same terms as all other fellow citizens. This is an account of the secular that can be defended against many religiously motivated critics of secularism. It avoids the objection that secularism (in some of its forms) can function just like a religion in the sense of providing fundamental convictions and values for its adherents. It would be as wrong to impose such a worldview on citizens of a state as it would be to impose a religious worldview. Equally it would be wrong to demand of all religiously motivated citizens that they refrain from the expression of religiously formulated opinions in public debate: those secularists who do so want the liberal state to abandon one of the key pillars of a liberal state in a pluralist society, the freedom of speech.

The second arena in the secular debates about secularity concerns the law, specifically, the interpretation by the European Court of Human Rights (ECtHR) of the provisions of the European convention concerning religious freedom. Ian Leigh has documented a tendency in the judgments of the ECtHR to endorse a radical secular conception of neutrality in decisions concerning religion, even though there is no mention of neutrality in the relevant articles of the convention.[36] The previous standard approach in the European Court's jurisprudence had relied on an understanding of neutrality as equality of respect, but this had shifted toward a view of neutrality as equidistance. Equality of respect had allowed the ECtHR to recognize the so-called margin of appreciation in each particular state's circumstances, in which there are differing accommodations of religion and of churches. Equality of respect had tolerated a positive attitude by the state toward religious communities without elevating any one church or religion to the status of established church. Equidistance, by contrast, conveyed a negative attitude of the state toward religion, reflecting more the American situation of constitutionally established separation than the complex European circumstances. Tacitly adopting the sense of neutrality as equidistance of the state from all churches and religions, the European Court was in danger of imposing a single model on the varied circumstances of European states.[37] Although Leigh documents that there is some evidence that the tendency has been halted, as for instance in the Grand Chamber's reversal of the Second Chamber's decisions regarding *Lautsi v. Italy*, it remains to be seen if this will be carried through in practice. Leigh writes, "Judge Power argued that '*Neutrality requires a pluralist approach on the part of the State, not a secularist one. It encourages respect for all world views rather than a preference for one.* To my mind, the [Second] Chamber judgment was striking in its failure to recognize that *secularism* (which was the applicant's preferred belief or world view) was, *in itself, one ideology among others. A preference for secularism* over alternative world views—whether religious, philosophical or otherwise—*is not a neutral option*' (para. 3, emphasis added)."[38]

The third secular debate is in the sociology of religion. Linda Woodhead, the renowned British sociologist of religion, comments on how an imperialistic secularism leads to distortions in the academic discourse when illiberal secularism is allowed to set the focus of discussion and the terms of the debate. Whenever the problems are so formulated that it appears as if religion were the main threat to liberalism, then the religious perspective is placed on the defensive, needing to justify itself but allowed to do so only in terms permitted by the secularist. Woodhead defends the compatibility of religion with liberalism and sees antireligious secularism as illiberal. Her principal target is the idea "that 'secular liberalism' is identical with liberalism."[39] She challenges what she sees as the key elements of secular liberalism, namely, the agenda to keep religion out of politics and to achieve a strict separation between the state and religion, confining religion to a purely private sphere.[40]

Woodhead's sociological approach summarizes the core values and principles of liberalism and locates individual freedom among its key ideas, stressing that individuals as sovereign choosers should be free to choose their religion and core convictions. She argues that historically and intellectually religious thinkers played an important role in the valuing of liberty and that in Britain today illiberal religion is the exception, not the norm. An antireligious secularism jeopardizes liberalism because it distracts from the real threats to freedom, as exemplified in the totalitarianisms of the twentieth century. "Illiberalism," she writes, "cannot be so neatly contained—as if our civil liberties were only under threat from religion. The danger of a radical secular ideology is not only that it mislocates the problem of illiberalism, but that in doing so it contributes to it. A richer understanding of a free society is not one in which either religion or secularism has a monopoly and seeks to exclude the other, but one in which both religious and non-religious people and institutions are able to choose, contribute, belong, express their opinions, debate and contest."[41] The question is not about the place of religion in a secular, pluralist society but instead how a liberal society can deal with illiberalism in its various forms, whether religious intolerance or antidemocratic ideologies.

CONCLUSION

These debates in philosophy, jurisprudence, and sociology provide evidence that Trainor's theological distinction between different forms of the secular has parallels in various nontheological disciplines. In every case there is a form of the secular that is capable of accommodating religion without being threatened by it. In political philosophy justificatory secularism establishes standards for legislators and judges to justify their enactments and rulings but does not require the same standards of restraint on the part of citizens and civil society. In jurisprudence the important principle of separation can be institutionalized in various ways, and it would be an unwarranted imposition to require all liberal states to interpret their stance as one of neutrality understood as equidistance from all religions. In the sociology of religion it is a distortion of the data to frame questions based on the assumption that religion is illiberal: the secularist stance that does so shows itself to be illiberal. Each of these contributions attempts to secure the entitlement of religion to a role in public life against tendencies to deny it that space in the name of secularism. They confirm, therefore, the relevance of Trainor and Beiner in allowing us to conclude that there is a version of the secular and its relation to religion that from the point of view of political philosophy is defensible and robust and that from the point of view of religion and theology can be justified and defended as appropriate for rule of states, in which religious communities and churches can thrive and can contribute richly to a pluralist society. This version of the secular is a potential partner in cooperation and is definitely not scary.

NOTES

1. Ronald Beiner, *Civil Religion: A Dialogue in the History of Political Philosophy* (Cambridge: Cambridge University Press, 2011); Brian T. Trainor, *Christ, Society and the State* (Adelaide: Australasian Theological Forum Press, 2010); Brian T. Trainor, "Augustine's Glorious City of God as Principle of the Political," *Heythrop Journal* 51 (2010): 543–53; Brian T. Trainor, "Augustine's 'Sacred Reign—Secular Rule' Conception of the State; a Bridge from the West's Foundational Roots to Its Post-Secular Destiny, and between 'The West' and 'The Rest,'" *Heythrop Journal* 56 (2015): 373–87.

2. Machiavelli, "The Prince," in *The Prince and Other Political Writings*, Selected and Translated by B. Penman (London: Dent, 1981).

3. Thomas Hobbes, *Leviathan* (Oxford: Oxford University Press, 1996).

4. Ibid., ch. 6.

5. William T. Cavanaugh, *Theopolitical Imagination* (London: T&T Clark, 2002).

6. Ibid., 35.

7. Ibid., 22.

8. Jean-Jacques Rousseau, *The Social Contract*, A New Translation by Christopher Betts (Oxford: Oxford University Press, 1994).

9. Beiner, *Civil Religion*, 82.

10. Ibid., 83.

11. Rowan Williams, "Politics and the Soul: A Reading of the *City of God*," *Milltown Studies* 19–20 (1987): 55–72.

12. Oliver O'Donovan and Joan Lockwood O'Donovan, "The Political Thought of 'City of God,'" in *Bonds of Imperfection: Christian Politics, Past and Present* (Grand Rapids, MI: Eerdmans, 2004).

13. Ibid., 55–56.

14. Trainor, "Augustine's Glorious City of God as Principle of the Political," 547.

15. Ibid., 549.

16. Patrick Riordan, *A Grammar of the Common Good* (London: Continuum, 2008).

17. Trainor, "Augustine's 'Sacred Reign—Secular Rule' Conception of the State," 375.

18. Ibid.

19. Glenn Hughes, "The Concept of Dignity in the Universal Declaration of Human Rights," *Journal of Religious Ethics* 39, no. 1 (2011): 1–24.

20. Mary Ann Glendon, *A World Made New: Eleanor Roosevelt and the Universal Declaration of Human Rights* (New York: Random House, 2001).

21. Hughes, "The Concept of Dignity."

22. John Rawls, *Political Liberalism* (New York: Columbia University Press, 1996).

23. Trainor, "Augustine's 'Sacred Reign—Secular Rule' Conception of the State," 381.

24. John Rawls, *The Law of Peoples with "The Idea of Public Reason Revisited"* (Cambridge, MA: Harvard University Press, 1999).

25. Nicholas Boyle, *2014: How to Survive the Next World Crisis* (London: Continuum, 2010).

26. Jason Ralph, *Defending the Society of States: Why America Opposes the International Criminal Court and Its Vision of World Society* (Oxford: Oxford University Press, 2007).

27. David Luban, "Preventive War," *Philosophy and Public Affairs* 32 (2004): 207–48.

28. Patrick Riordan, *Global Ethics and Global Common Goods* (London: Bloomsbury, 2015).

29. Rousseau, *Social Contract*.

30. Rawls, *Political Liberalism*.

31. Cécile Laborde, "Justificatory Secularism," in *Religion in a Liberal State: Cross-Disciplinary Reflections* (Cambridge: Cambridge University Press, 2013), 164–86, at 167.

32. Ibid., 185.

33. Rawls, *Law of Peoples*, 132.

34. Ibid., 143.

35. Nicholas Wolterstorff, "The Role of Religion in Decision and Discussion of Political Issues," in *Religion in the Public Square*, ed. Robert Audi and Nicholas Wolterstorff (London: Rowman & Littlefield, 1997), 67–120, at 81.

36. Ian Leigh, "The European Court of Human Rights and Religious Neutrality," in *Religion in a Liberal State*, ed. Gavin D'Costa, Malcolm Evans, Tariq Modood, and Julian Rivers (Cambridge: Cambridge University Press, 2013), 38–66, at 39.

37. Ibid., 62.

38. Ibid., 61.

39. Linda Woodhead, "Liberal Religion and Illiberal Secularism," in D'Costa et al., *Religion in a Liberal State*, 93–116.

40. Ibid., 95–96.

41. Ibid., 112–13.

Epilogue

CORNELIUS J. CASEY

MANNA FOR A DESERT WALK

Comme la manne pour le peuple d'Israël, ainsi, pour chaque
génération chrétienne, l'Eucharistie est la nourriture indispensable
qui la soutient tandis qu'elle traverse le désert de ce monde, asséché
par les systèmes idéologiques et économiques qui ne promeuvent
pas la vie, mais lui portent atteinte; un monde où domine la logique
du pouvoir et de l'avoir plutôt que celle du service et de l'amour; un
monde où triomphe souvent la culture de la violence et de la mort.

Pape Benoit XVI, 7 Juin 2007

These words greet the visitor stepping from the street into the Cathedral
of Notre Dame in Luxembourg: "Like the manna for the people of Israel,
the Eucharist for each Christian generation is the indispensable nourish-
ment that sustains them as they cross the desert of this world, parched

by the ideological and economic systems which do not promote life but rather humiliate it. It is a world where the logic of power and possessions prevails rather than that of service and love, a world where the culture of violence and death is frequently triumphant."[1] This startling proclamation could be taken to suggest that *out there*, in *that city*, is a complexity of ideologies sterile for human flourishing, a hostile environment for the project of Christian living. In this case, *that city* is Luxembourg, one of the principal financial powerhouses of the contemporary market economy. There is a journey to be made. It is a journey away from the city.

This way of setting the coordinates for the relationship between church and society has had, from antiquity and down the centuries, interesting and respected supporters. It brings its own proper illumination. It is represented, for example, by the early monastic movement, considerable numbers of men and women who, deciding that the Christian life could not be lived well in cities, moved out into the deserts of Egypt. This was not because they wanted to turn to nature, or were charmed by the beauty of the desert, but simply because the desert was not the city. They traveled to the desert to move away from society, away from the culture of the city, "a world where the culture of violence and death is frequently triumphant."[2]

The narrative is that the human world had become an idolatrous society through and through. The world, in this view, is still in the power of the Prince of this world. True, the Prince of this world has been cast down and defeated in the death of Jesus, but that does not mean there has been the complete collapse of the old system. The old system is still out there in the city crouched like a lion waiting to devour you. If you get lured in, perhaps fascinated by its pretense of self-improvement, it will gobble you up. You will end up working for the system, for "ideological and economic systems which do not promote life but rather humiliate it." The church, a pilgrim people, must not be tempted to settle there. It does not have here a lasting city. *Fuga mundi.* Flee. The Eucharist is food for the journey because it brings a foretaste of the kingdom of God, the kingdom of *caritas*.

Fuga mundi is a signpost, an illumination. The spectacular route pioneered by the early monks of the Egyptian desert is also the route taken by the Celtic monks making their way to Sceilig Mhichíl off the west coast of Ireland. Their communities lasted for many centuries, from (perhaps) the seventh century to the time when the settlement was abandoned in the twelfth century. Carthusian monks traveled this route, high on the French Alps, when they founded La Grande Chartreuse in 1084. From the point of view of all these Christians (and many more like them through the centuries) there wasn't any point in being concerned about the world and its problems. It was not their concern to change the world. Their task was to change themselves in a community guided by the Holy Spirit. This is a very different thing from trying to bring about a just world order. It is an illusion, they might have said, to think that any such thing could be done, and, perhaps, a sinful vanity besides.[3]

The proper illumination these movements bring is that the church is not a political project. It is not a project to bring about a just world order. These Christians travel away from the city because in the Eucharist they had come to realize that Jesus is the signifier of all human history, the single stark signifier that tells what it is all about. Jesus spoke out for love and justice in obedience to the one he called his Father. He was done to death, but death did not have the last word and the only real hope for human flourishing was born there.

If you stay in the city, or even linger there, the city will eventually remake you in its image. So these Christians leave in the hope of being remade in the image of the stone rejected by the builder, destined to become the cornerstone of human flourishing.

Some critics of modernity stake out a similar strategy for our times. Alasdair MacIntyre in his celebrated work, *After Virtue*, set out to study the nature of moral community and moral judgment in distinctively modern societies. His conclusion was that modern society, our society, cannot hope to achieve moral consensus. Modern politics cannot be a matter of genuine moral consensus. Does it follow, he asked, that we are led on to a generalized pessimism? Not at all, he said. There are certain parallels between our own age and the epoch in which the Roman Empire declined into the Dark Ages. At that juncture some people of goodwill turned aside from the task of shoring up Roman civility, and instead set out to construct new forms of community that might survive the coming ages of barbarism and darkness. MacIntyre suggests that for some time now we in our age have reached a similar crucial turning point.

What matters at this stage is the construction of local forms of community within which civility and the intellectual and moral life can be sustained through the new dark ages which are already upon us. This time however the barbarians are not waiting beyond the frontiers; they have already been governing us for quite some time. And it is our lack of consciousness of this that constitutes part of our predicament. We are waiting not for a Godot, but for another— doubtless very different—St Benedict.[4]

It is against this backdrop, of a pretty radical refutation of an opti- mistic diagnosis of our social cultural orders, that some writers in this volume develop suggestions for a more authentic ecclesial strategy. The secular might not be scary, but contemporary consumerist liberalism cer- tainly is. This is the case argued in the work of Patrick J. Deneen. The liberalism of contemporary pluralist society is a skein of cultural (or anti- cultural) self-fashioning that is both alienating and all-encompassing. Its pretense of offering a welcoming, tolerant home for Christian traditions is false, deceptive, and dangerous. The vocation of the church is not to heed the siren calls of the liberalist and consumerist order, a social order that in truth is not pluralist at all but rather a pitiless global monoculture. The best strategy is "to turn aside" from the task of shoring up modernity's civility. The church cannot be merely a corrective or a balm for our age.

William T. Cavanaugh argues that the supremacy of choice, option- ality, as co-opted to the purposes of consumerist economy and culture, is so dominant that it now constructs our subjectivity. It has the hege- mony. It produces its own forms of conformity, hierarchy, and power. It cuts off routes to deeper human freedoms and deeper human flourish- ing. Both writers emphazise that the church must leave behind the world of imposed consensus. It must always strive to create alternative kinds of community that better facilitate living the gospel.

"Every political regime stands under the judgement of the Cross," writes Terry Eagleton.[5] This is a kind of commentary on John 18:23. There Jesus says, "My kingdom is not of this world." Mere improvement in the present situation will not bring about this kingdom. All Christian moral outlook stands under this judgment. However, the ethical implica- tions are complex, not singular. Indeed, there is often more than one set of such ethical implications. It is possible and it is fully consistent with this judgment to see or to try to see, or to try to learn to see, that our present world, even though it is indeed "parched by the ideological and economic systems that do not promote life but rather humiliate it," is nonetheless pregnant with the future, with the world to come. This is precisely the vocation of the church, to try to give visibility to this truth. Under the judgment of the cross the church has learned of God's outpouring of the Spirit in the world (not just in the church). Some early Christians fled the city in order to distance themselves from its violence and the hegemony of its cultural tropes and to find their salvation in the blood of the Lamb. Their witness is revered in the long narrative of the church. There is another trajectory that would take Christian travelers precisely back into the city, knowing full well that it is parched by alienating ideologies. Fostered by Christian hope they would seek there signs and pledges of the future world, especially among "those who are poor and afflicted in any way" (*GS* 1). It is this trajectory that was most favored in the reflections of *Gaudium et Spes*: "Although we must be careful to distinguish earthly progress clearly from the increase of the kingdom of Christ, such progress is of vital concern to the kingdom of God, insofar as it can contribute to the better ordering of human society" (*GS* 39).

In this perspective Massimo Faggioli reflects that a radical withdrawal of the church from the public square would mean losing the platform that allows the church to speak in favor and on behalf of those who are excluded from the economic system. The last best hope that the truly marginalized have would be dissipated. Coming from another angle, Patrick Riordan maintains that it is surely part of the ecclesial calling to remain open to the secular, positioned there to give visibility to the presence of the Spirit and the grace of redemption. J. Bryan Hehir recalls that Pope John XXIII encouraged such engagement in *Pacem in Terris* and that Pope John Paul II in *Laborem Exercens* described human work in all its forms as cooperation with God's creative activity. In these authors it is a genuine dimension of church responsibility to work with pluralism intelligently and effectively. Pluralism is here to stay.

Who speaks for the church pilgrim in this journey through and with contemporary cultures? The loci of authority call for attention. The Second Vatican Council had discerned that the wisdom of *sensus fidelium* is an important resource. It too is the work of the Spirit, alongside the other gifts of leadership and authority in the ecclesial community. How can this be properly conceived? How can it be properly retrieved, properly deployed? The better our theological understanding of the loci of authority, claims Fáinche Ryan, the better will be our discernment of the role of church in pluralist societies, and the more intelligent and the more effective will be our engagement.

In the end, it is as the visibility of Christian hope that the church has special relevance to our age. Visibility includes the issues of institutional shape and sociological form. In an age when optionality pervades the social order, there is a temptation for the church to reconceive itself as a sort of club for its voluntary membership. It is a temptation to be resisted at all costs. The church is not a club. It is the sacrament of humankind moving toward its horizon in the kingdom. Yet change is afoot. Failure to find appropriate social form and structure is probably already undermining or obstructing ecclesial vitality, Hans Joas argues. This is a formidable challenge for the church in our time.

DOES HISTORY RHYME WITH HOPE?

The Christian moral and political outlook is drawn from contact with the future. As such the Christian moral and political outlook is based essentially on the virtue of hope. The ecclesial community is schooled in hope, especially in the Eucharist, a foretaste and pledge of the future kingdom. Every baptized person is, in principle, sent out to search for signs of the kingdom, hunting for the pledges of the future in the present.

The logic of hope carries its participants in a diversity of trajectories. What remains certain and clear throughout is that Christian hope is not optimism. "We are not optimists," writes the theologian Herbert McCabe, "we do not present a lovely vision of the world which everyone is expected to fall in love with. We simply have, wherever we are, some small local task to do on the side of justice, for the poor."[6] We can make moves toward a better world on the side of justice, for the poor. The improved reality of our efforts would not yet, of course, be the kingdom. It would be a better picture of it, foreshadowing it in some way: "Far from diminishing our concern to develop this earth, the expectation of a new earth should spur us on, for it is here that the body of a new human family grows, foreshadowing in some way the age that is to come" (GS 39).

Such efforts risk defeat and failure. In 1968 when the Conference of Latin American Bishops, meeting in Medellín, agreed that the church should take a preferential option for the poor, this gave a great visibility of Christian hope. The goal was to liberate people from the institutionalized violence of poverty. When, in the spirit of Medellín, numerous men and women created Christian base communities, they were forging signs of hope, pledges of the future kingdom. Such efforts risked defeat and failure. The story of the movement that became known as liberation theology bears plentiful witness to such risk—and at once stands as a great witness to Christian hope. This is a kind of hope that can risk defeat for it is based on the promise of resurrection. It journeys alongside defeat, and yet no matter how desolate the situation hope is the last word.

There remains the mysterious interlinking between hope and history. The poet Seamus Heaney writes:

> History says, don't hope
> On this side of the grave
> But then, once in a lifetime
> The longed-for tidal wave
> Of justice can rise up
> And hope and history rhyme.[7]

NOTES

1. Pope Benedict XVI, Homily of His Holiness Benedict XVI, Solemnity of Corpus Christi, Thursday, June 7, 2007, https://w2.vatican.va/content/benedict-xvi /en/homilies/2007/documents/hf_ben-xvi_hom_20070607_corpus-christi.html.

2. These points are developed in Herbert McCabe, *God Still Matters* (London: Continuum, 2002), 88, 89.

3. Herbert McCabe, *God Matters* (London: Continuum, 2002), 87.

4. Alasdair MacIntyre, *After Virtue* (London: Duckworth, 1981), 245.

5. Terry Eagleton, *Radical Sacrifice* (New Haven, CT: Yale University Press, 2018), 54.

6. Herbert McCabe, *God, Christ and Us* (London: Continuum, 2003), 14.

7. Seamus Heaney, *The Cure at Troy: A Version of Sophocles's "Philoctetes"* (London: Faber and Faber, 1990), 77.

CONTRIBUTORS

Cornelius J. Casey was the inaugural director of the Loyola Institute, Trinity College Dublin. Previously he was president of the Milltown Institute of Theology and Philosophy and director of Kimmage Mission Institute, Dublin. From 1999 to 2008 he served as provincial of the Irish Redemptorist Congregation. His degrees are from San Anselmo, Rome, and Oxford. Casey has lectured extensively in India, Ireland, and the United Kingdom. His research interests include the theology of Thomas Aquinas and current issues in ecclesiology.

William T. Cavanaugh is director of the Center for World Catholicism and Intercultural Theology and professor of Catholic studies at DePaul University. His degrees are from the University of Notre Dame, Cambridge, and Duke. He is coeditor of the journal *Modern Theology* and the author of seven books, including *The Myth of Religious Violence: Secular Ideology and the Roots of Modern Conflict* (Oxford, 2009) and, most recently, *Field Hospital: The Church's Engagement with a Wounded World* (Eerdmans, 2016). He has lectured on six continents, and his writings have been published in twelve languages.

Patrick J. Deneen is professor of constitutional law at the University of Notre Dame. He holds a BA in English literature and a PhD in political science from Rutgers University. His teaching and writing interests focus on the history of political thought, American political thought, religion and politics, and literature and politics. His published books include *Democratic Faith* (Princeton, 2005), *The Democratic Soul* (ed.) (Kentucky, 2011), and *Conserving America? Thoughts on Present Discontents* (St. Augustine Press, 2016).

Terry Eagleton is Distinguished Professor of English Literature, University of Lancaster. He is the author of more than fifty books spanning the fields of literary theory, postmodernism, politics, ideology, and religion. He lives in Northern Ireland. His publications include *Reason, Faith and Revolution* (Yale, 2009), *Hope without Optimism* (Yale, 2015), and *Materialism* (Yale, 2016).

Massimo Faggioli is professor in the Department of Theology and Religious Studies at Villanova University and is contributing writer to *Commonweal*. His books and essays have been published in ten languages. His most recent publications include *The Rising Laity: Ecclesial Movements since Vatican II* (Paulist Press, 2016), *Catholicism and Citizenship: Political Cultures of the Church in the Twenty-First Century* (Liturgical Press, 2017), *La onda larga del Vaticano II: Por un nuevo posconcilio* (Universidad Alberto Hurtado, Santiago de Chile, 2017).

Bryan J. Hehir is Parker Gilbert Montgomery Professor of the Practice of Religion and Public Life at Harvard University's John F. Kennedy School of Government. Previously he served on the staff of the US Conference of Catholic Bishops. He served on the faculty of Georgetown University and the Harvard Divinity School. His research and writing focus on ethics and foreign policy and the role of religion in world politics and in American society. His writings include "The Moral Measurement of War: A Tradition of Continuity and Change," "Military Intervention and National Sovereignty," "Strategic Logic and the Killing of Civilians," and "Theology, Social Teaching and Catholic Charities."

Hans Joas is Ernst Troeltsch Professor for the Sociology of Religion at the Humboldt University of Berlin and Professor of Sociology and Social Thought at the University of Chicago. Among his recent book publications in English are *The Sacredness of the Person: A New Genealogy of Human Rights* (Georgetown, 2013), *War in Social Thought: Hobbes to the Present* (Princeton, 2013), and *Faith as an Option: Possible Futures for Christianity* (Stanford, 2014).

Patrick Riordan, SJ, is Fellow in Political Philosophy and Catholic Social Thought at Campion Hall, Oxford. He is a member of the Heythrop

Institute: Religion and Society. He was formerly president of Milltown Institute of Theology and Philosophy in Dublin. In addition to his publications on the common good, recent articles have dealt with human dignity and human rights, restorative justice in penal policy, and the proposed legislation for the autonomous region of Muslim Mindanao in the Philippines. His publications include *Global Ethics and Global Common Goods* (Bloomsbury, 2015) and *Recovering Common Goods* (Veritas, 2017).

Fáinche Ryan, Fellow of Trinity College Dublin, is director of the Loyola Institute, Trinity College Dublin, and a lecturer in systematic theology. Her doctorate is from the University of St. Thomas Aquinas (Angelicum), Rome. She was president of the Irish Theological Association from 2012 to 2017. Her current research interest lies in the area of questions of ecclesiology and leadership. Her publications include *Formation in Holiness: Thomas Aquinas on Sacra Scriptura* (Peeters Leuven, 2007), *Karl Rahner: Theologian for the Twenty-First Century* (ed. with Pádraic Conway) (Peter Lang, 2010), and *The Eucharist: What Do We Believe?* (Veritas, 2012).

INDEX

Lightning Source UK Ltd.
Milton Keynes UK
UKHW022057140120
356948UK00005B/161/P